Nft

Using Crypto currencies on the Block chain

(An Essential Guide to Understanding and Investing in Non-fungible Tokens and Crypto Art)

Edward Carden

Published By **Cathy Nedrow**

Edward Carden

All Rights Reserved

Nft: Using Crypto currencies on the Block chain
(An Essential Guide to Understanding and
Investing in Non-fungible Tokens and Crypto Art)

ISBN 978-1-7772262-9-9

No part of this guidebook shall be reproduced in any form without permission in writing from the publisher except in the case of brief quotations embodied in critical articles or reviews.

Legal & Disclaimer

The information contained in this book is not designed to replace or take the place of any form of medicine or professional medical advice. The information in this book has been provided for educational & entertainment purposes only.

The information contained in this book has been compiled from sources deemed reliable, and it is accurate to the best of the Author's knowledge; however, the Author cannot guarantee its accuracy and validity and cannot be held liable for any errors or omissions. Changes are periodically made to this book. You must consult your doctor or get professional medical advice before using any of the suggested remedies, techniques, or information in this book.

Table Of Contents

Chapter 1: Block Chain And Crypto Overseas Money

Imagine stepping into a grocery save to buy some stuff and need to pay by means of manner of sending cash to the store proprietor's account. Many things ought to pass wrong at the same time as on the lookout for to deliver the coins; there are probably technical system faults because of systems malfunctioning or machines now not jogging. The save owner's account might have been hacked - as an example; there can be identity robbery or denial of provider attack. More so, you could have exceeded your transfer restrict for the day. However, in all, the primary aspect of failure is established to the conventional banks.

Now, recollect you need to do a similar transaction through your Bit coin app. You accumulate a notification indicating in case you really need to exchange thru Bit coin. If yes, then the method starts. This tool confirms your identity; exams whether or not you have got that amount for your account to make that transaction, and so on. Once the ones necessities are met, the transfer is performed, and the person gets it from their account right away. This entire manner takes a couple of minutes. This clearly technique crypto currency breaks all boundaries and solves all the issues associated with moving and receiving coins. With this, there aren't any limits to the price range you may transfer, and your account can never be hacked. That's the big difference crypto currency is bringing to the economic panorama.

Before we unpack more blessings you advantage the use of crypto currency, allows communicate what crypto currency technique and the way it is related to block chain.

What Exactly Is Crypto currency?

The word crypto currency derives its call from the usage of cryptography requirements in minting virtual coins. These coins are increasingly well-known as opportunity manner of transaction inside the virtual global. Examples are Ethereum, Bitcoin, Litecoin, and plenty of others. Cryptocurrencies are popularly referred to as crypto or digital forex because of the truth they may be only to be had in digital shape and are used for transactions inside the virtual global. One precise trouble approximately these currencies is that they remove the want to make transactions with bodily coins. More so, no matter the truth that they may be to be had online, you can use them to make physical purchases.

Unlike the physical cash that's below the manage of a government and published satisfactory with the useful resource of corporations legal with the aid of manner of them, numerous organizations and those promote or mint cash and motive them to to be had for clients and buyers.

Another must-say feature of cryptocurrency is that it doesn't require a financial organisation or any financial corporation to confirm any transaction or transfer of charge range. All transactions are established and recorded on a blockchain, that is an unchangeable, secured ledger in which transactions are recorded and tracked. It is an area wherein assets are secured in opposition to hacking or theft.

However, in phrases of blockchain, there's more than what has been stated earlier than. So, it's miles vitally vital we find out blockchain and its interrelatedness with virtual forex.

What is a Blockchain?

In explaining what blockchain is, it's miles first-rate to borrow the phrases of Buchi Okoro, who's the founding father of Quidax, one of the extremely good crypto change organizations. He says, "Imagine a e-book wherein you write down the whole lot you invest in each day. Each net page is just like a block, and the whole ebook, a tough and rapid of pages, is a blockchain." In essence, Okoro technique with blockchain, each user or investor has their precise duplicate of this ebook to installation a unified transaction report. Each new transaction, because it takes region, is mechanically registered, and each reproduction of the blockchain receives up to date due to the current-day information, making all facts up to date, accurate, and equal.

Getting a clue from that, we're able to simply talk with a blockchain as an open dispensed ledger in which all transactions are saved in code. In exercise, a blockchain is a few issue like a checkbook it is shared throughout numerous systems round the world. Transactions are well stored in 'blocks' which may be because it have to be associated together on a 'chain' of preceding transactions. So, as new transactions (blocks) are made, they'll be connected together on a sequence with preceding transactions to hold it up to date. This, of path, is a first rate way to save you fraud since every patron includes a totally unique validation method referred to as evidence-of-stake or proof-of-art work. This validation technique definitely contains the identification of the proprietor and stops others from getting unrestricted or unauthorized get proper of access to to the account.

Brief History and Evolution of Blockchain Technology

Now that we've got got talked in quick about cryptocurrencies and blockchain era, the subsequent element is to provide a brief historic evaluation of blockchain technology. This is useful because it lets in to tune the improvement the generation has made so far and the way reliable it's been over the years.

At the height of the economic demanding situations in 2008, an brilliant technological development occurred. This technology would possibly no longer handiest trade the whole financial panorama; it brings a complete trade that transforms the manner we relate with cash and breaks the limitations related to making transactions. This era is none apart from Blockchain technology, a brand new digital coins system that is a definitely peer-to-peer machine with out third-celebration involvement.

The generation turned into first defined via famend scientists Scott Stornetta and Stuart Haber in their studies in 1991. The particular idea changed into to increase a computationally realistic answer for timestamping digital documents just so they could not be tampered with or backdated. However, they sooner or later evolved a machine the use of the idea of cryptographically stable chains of blocks to file the time stamped document.

After that try, Merkle Trees were protected into the format someday in 1992, which made the cryptographic end up extra inexperienced with the beneficial useful resource of allowing extraordinary documents to be stored proper right into a block. Merkle Trees are used to save more than one information, with every data being gathered from the previous one.

In 2004, cryptographic expert and computer scientist Hal Finney added a device called

Reusable Proof of Work (RPoW) for instance of virtual coins. Many humans regarded this attempt as one of the maximum huge early steps within the annal of virtual currencies. This system operates via receiving a non-exchangeable or a non-fungible Hashcash-based totally proof of exertions token in return, that is with out problem transferred from one individual to some distinctive.

However, in 2008, Satoshi Nakamoto came up with the concept of allotted blockchains. He advanced a totally precise manner to dam the prevailing ones without having the signature or approval of any relied on occasions. The changed model ought to encompass a strong information of records exchanges. It makes use of a peer-to-peer community to verify every transaction and timestamp. The system is self-managed. Therefore, a central authority is not required. These advancements have been so particular and beneficial that they made blockchain the backbone that gives strength for the survival of digital currencies. Today, the layout serves because the important public ledger in which all transactions are saved in the virtual space.

The evolution of blockchain has been amazing, promising, and steady. Satoshi Nakamoto used the paintings chain and block one after the other in his paper but subsequently obtained traction as a single phrase - blockchain in 2016. Recently, the document length of the crypto blockchain that houses the entire transaction has expanded from 20 GB to a hundred GB.

Cryptocurrencies and their role in DeFi and NFTs

In modern instances, the decentralized finance (DeFi) landscape has become famous due to the manner it motives a main shift inside the monetary location. Of route, a foreign money it is major in this outstanding stride is Bitcoin, the region's first and most famend virtual forex. The have an effect on of this foreign exchange goes beyond its role as digital cash, as it has prolonged its place and appears in the realm of NFTs and DeFi.

Undoubtedly, Bitcoin is shaping the worlds of NFTs and DeFi and making prepared each for future increase.

Before we discover Bitcoin's involvement in DeFi, it is right to set up a smooth information of DeFi. DeFi is clearly using digital currencies and blockchain era to recreate conventional financial systems in a decentralized way. DeFi dreams to provide unrestricted, permissionless, open, and inclusive financial offerings with the purpose of putting off the need for physical financial institutions like banks. Most DeFi programs are used for truely all of the sports that banks carry out for their users. Financial sports sports together with buying and selling, borrowing, lending, and others are accomplished through clever contracts, allowing clients to gain unrestricted get entry to and complete manipulate over their funds.

The incorporation of cryptocurrency like Bitcoin into the DeFi and NFTs worldwide brings forth numerous novel opportunities.

For example, Bitcoin's unique functions, together with liquidity, emblem, giant adoption, and potential to make secured transactions, have made NFTs and DeFi appealing to DeFi clients and artwork creators.

In DeFi, Bitcoin is used as a Store of Value, which makes it constant for DeFi contributors who would love to develop their wealth. DeFi systems have abilties that permit users to lock their price range for a few intervals. Also, Bitcoin's liquidity function and high marketplace capitalization make it useful as a treasured collateral asset internal DeFi. Additionally, considering the reality that lending and borrowing are number one sports activities in the economic sphere, Bitcoin's incorporation into DeFi lending protocols makes it feasible for DeFi members to get right of entry to lending and borrowing services as banks provide them. More so, Bitcoin's integration has introduced peer-to-peer purchasing for and promoting on DeFi, making the people revel in decentralized exchanges without intermediaries. Lastly, Bitcoin's integration offers room for staking and yield farming, making it possible for DeFi participants to make passive profits virtually with the resource of maintaining their finances in particular protocols or certainly with the useful resource of supplying liquidity. This is why many people take delivery of as real with that Bitcoin is beginning to make its presence felt in this digital area.

Chapter 2: Understanding Decentralized Finance

In a worldwide this is increasingly related and digital, the economic landscape isn't always evidence in opposition to transformation. Decentralized finance, extra normally known as DeFi, is a term that has captured the imagination of seasoned consumers and those new to finance. At its coronary heart, DeFi is an impressive and bold agency. Defi seeks to recreate and enhance traditional financial offerings at the same time as dismantling the traditional systems of banks and other centralized establishments. This economic machine is open, transparent, and peer-to-peer, completed via the virtual ledger era of blockchain that underpins cryptocurrencies like Bitcoin and Ethereum. In this chapter, we are able to explore the very essence of DeFi, its principles, and desires. We will delve into its historic emergence and the crucial tendencies that have brought about its speedy growth. From Ethereum's smart contracts to the upward push of decentralized exchanges, this economic smash will lay the inspiration for statistics the DeFi panorama.

We may also explore the vital aspect additives and protocols that make DeFi tick. Smart contracts, decentralized exchanges, lending systems, yield farming, tokenization, and oracles, each of these constructing blocks performs a crucial feature within the DeFi surroundings. Understanding how they feature and have interaction is essential for absolutely everyone in search of to navigate this exciting new world of finance.

But DeFi isn't without its disturbing situations. With top notch energy comes remarkable duty, and DeFi is no exception. It faces ability pitfalls, from the vulnerabilities of smart contracts to the ever-evolving regulatory panorama. Market volatility, a lack of character-nice interfaces, and the looming specter of scams and fraud pose massive dangers that customers need to be aware about. Let's begin by way of way of exploring what Defi technique.

What is DeFi

Decentralized finance, generally referred to as DeFi, refers to a innovative monetary device built on blockchain era that seeks to recreate and enhance conventional economic offerings, doing away with the want for intermediaries like banks and specific centralized institutions.

DeFi desires to take away centralized government and intermediaries, giving clients complete manipulate over their financial assets and picks. Transactions arise without delay amongst buddies on a decentralized network, lowering the chance of censorship or 0.33-celebration manipulation. DeFi prioritizes transparency thru the usage of blockchain technology. All transactions and records are recorded on a public ledger accessible to absolutely everyone. Users can verify the integrity of financial operations, fostering trust. DeFi strives to make financial services handy to a broader worldwide population. Its permissionless nature manner that everyone with a web connection can participate, doubtlessly presenting banking offerings to the unbanked and underbanked.

The Emergence of DeFi

DeFi, short for Decentralized Finance, represents a groundbreaking evolution in the monetary place, rooted within the broader cryptocurrency and blockchain revolution. Its improvement may be traced again to numerous pivotal milestones:

Ethereum and the Advent of Smart Contracts (2015): A foundational 2d inside the information of DeFi have turn out to be the release of Ethereum in 2015. Ethereum introduced clever contracts - self-executing code that allows monetary agreements and allows automation in DeFi.

The ICO Boom (2017): In 2017, Initial Coin Offerings (ICOs) emerged as a well-known fundraising mechanism for blockchain obligations. These ICOs allowed startups to elevate capital via issuing their tokens or cash. This fundraising frenzy injected high-quality capital into the cryptocurrency place, developing an environment ripe for innovation.

Rise of Decentralized Exchanges (DEXs): The DeFi panorama accelerated with the emergence of decentralized exchanges (DEXs) like Uniswap and Kyber Network. These structures supplied users with the potential to trade cryptocurrencies right away with each other, sidestepping the need for centralized exchanges. DEXs offered a more strong and obvious way to alternate virtual assets and have come to be a middle problem of DeFi infrastructure.

These key tendencies laid the muse for the DeFi ecosystem, placing the level for a decentralized and transparent monetary tool that operates without intermediaries. The subsequent boom of DeFi systems, lending and borrowing protocols, liquidity provision mechanisms, and modern economic gadget proven the functionality of blockchain technology to reshape the monetary business enterprise and offer clients greater control and inclusivity in their economic affairs.

Key Components and Protocols of DeFi

Smart Contracts

Smart contracts are self-executing pieces of code that play a critical function in DeFi. They automate and put in force economic agreements with out the need for intermediaries. Smart contracts execute predefined situations, in conjunction with the switch of belongings, whilst unique triggers are met. Smart contracts moreover ensure take into account and transparency via removing the need for 1/three-birthday celebration intermediaries in monetary transactions.

Decentralized Exchanges (DEXs):

DEXs are systems that permit peer-to-peer cryptocurrency searching for and promoting without the involvement of centralized intermediaries. Users can exchange one cryptocurrency for every exclusive right away, the use of liquidity swimming swimming pools and automated market-making algorithms. DEXs provide multiplied protection, reduced fees, and extra manipulate over assets.

Lending and Borrowing Platforms:

DeFi gives lending and borrowing structures, which encompass Aave and Compound, that be part of lenders and borrowers at the same time as no longer having conventional banks. Users can lend their virtual belongings in alternate for interest, and borrowers can get admission to loans with the useful resource of providing collateral. Interest prices are frequently decided via manner of supply and get in touch with for, offering possibilities for each passive income and liquidity.

Yield Farming and Liquidity Provision:

Participating in yield farming and liquidity provision approach contributing belongings to liquidity swimming swimming swimming pools on DeFi systems and earning rewards in go again. These swimming swimming pools are used for decentralized searching for and selling, and customers reap rewards via governance tokens or costs. Yield farming has emerged as a famous method for producing returns in the DeFi place.

Tokenization

Tokenization consists of representing conventional property, together with actual assets or shares, as digital tokens at the blockchain. Traditional belongings are transformed into blockchain tokens, making them with out troubles transferable and divisible. This way opens up opportunities for fractional ownership, multiplied liquidity, and simpler global trading of previously illiquid belongings.

Oracles

Oracles bridge the blockchain global and the real international with the aid of providing outside data to smart contracts. Oracles fetch real-international information, collectively with inventory prices, climate records, or sports activities sports activities ratings, and feed it into clever contracts. This permits DeFi applications to make decisions based totally on actual-international activities, growing the form of possible use instances.

Advantages of Using DeFi

Decentralized Finance (DeFi) gives some of compelling benefits, making it a transformative stress in the monetary international. Here are the important element blessings of the usage of DeFi:

Financial Inclusion

DeFi can provide monetary services to parents which are unbanked or underbanked, in particular those in regions with limited get entry to to traditional banking infrastructure. With the assist of honestly a web connection, each person can take part in DeFi, which allows them to maintain, make investments, borrow, and get right of entry to monetary services that have been previously unavailable to them.

Security and Transparency

Blockchain technology underpinning DeFi offers a excessive level of protection and transparency. Transactions and information are recorded on a public ledger, making them immutable and auditable. Smart contracts, at the same time as nicely designed and audited, make certain that agreements are done as intended, reducing the danger of fraud and disputes.

Control and Ownership

DeFi gives clients entire manage over their assets. There's no want for intermediaries like banks or brokerage companies, which often workout manipulate over purchaser debts. Users are in charge of their non-public keys and may have interaction with DeFi systems right away, doing away with counterparty risk.

High Liquidity

DeFi systems, collectively with decentralized exchanges (DEXs) and liquidity pools, offer excessive liquidity for masses cryptocurrencies. Users can speedy and without troubles trade or get admission to their assets with out relying on centralized exchanges. Liquidity vendors are incentivized to preserve those markets well-capitalized, ensuring sufficient buying and selling possibilities.

Innovation and Accessibility

DeFi is a hotbed of innovation, with developers constantly developing new monetary equipment, structures, and protocols. This innovation extends to regions like decentralized derivatives, prediction markets, and decentralized identity. The open nature of DeFi allows honestly every person to contribute, ensuing in speedy development and the non-stop improvement of recent monetary solutions.

Challenges of Using DeFi

It's critical to understand the capability risks and annoying conditions that encompass the evolving DeFi area notwithstanding its severa blessings.

Smart Contract Vulnerabilities

Smart contracts, despite the fact that effective, can contain coding mistakes or vulnerabilities that hackers can also make the maximum. These vulnerabilities can motive financial losses for users. Bugs or weaknesses in clever contracts can bring about accidental moves, together with losing price range. Proper auditing and code evaluate are essential to mitigate this chance.

Regulatory and Legal Concerns

The regulatory environment for DeFi stays evolving and may variety significantly with the useful useful resource of jurisdiction. Users also can come upon criminal issues approximately taxation, securities guidelines, and anti-cash laundering (AML) compliance.

Regulatory adjustments and enforcement movements may additionally impact the operation of DeFi structures.

Lack of User-Friendly Interfaces

DeFi systems frequently have complex person interfaces that may be daunting for inexperienced ladies and men. The individual experience and onboarding system can be hard, probably deterring mainstream adoption. Improved character interfaces and educational sources are needed to make DeFi handy to a broader goal market.

Market Volatility

DeFi operates in the cryptocurrency marketplace, acknowledged for its charge volatility. Users can also face super fee fluctuations in their virtual assets, affecting the price of collateral utilized in lending or borrowing. It's critical to be prepared for market volatility and manipulate chance as a end result.

Scams and Fraud

DeFi's open and permissionless nature can enchantment to awful actors and fraudulent schemes. Users have to be careful of phishing attacks, faux DeFi structures, and Ponzi schemes that promise immoderate returns. Engaging in due diligence, using relied on systems, and verifying the legitimacy of initiatives can assist customers keep away from scams.

Impermanent Loss

Liquidity carriers in DeFi systems can enjoy impermanent loss, which takes location whilst the value of their property in a liquidity pool diverges from protecting the ones assets outside the pool. It's a danger related to offering liquidity, and it could cause decreased returns in comparison to in truth preserving assets.

Chapter 3: Popular Defi Platforms And Projects

It isn't out of area now to say that you understand, like most human beings, what virtual currencies are, or at the least have observe approximately blockchain era and what DeFi is all about. This expertise is essential as it provides the idea for what you analyze in this e-book. However, on this economic damage, the emphasis is going to be on DeFi structures and duties which is probably presently inflicting a buzz within the virtual place.

DeFi has end up one of the maximum up to date and an thrilling region to focus on inside the virtual marketplace location these days. With new DeFi obligations coming into the virtual sphere daily and considering the capability that DeFi has to convert the area for the higher, plus the upward push inside the style of humans exploring the monetary options it gives, specially prolonged-term investment, is the purpose why gaining knowledge of about DeFi structures and projects a need to for absolutely everybody who absolutely wants to find out the virtual place.

Just as it's far received inside the traditional banking gadget, DeFi initiatives try to provide regular financial services, along aspect economic financial savings payments, loans, and asset exchanges to account holders. However, this affiliation differs from the traditional banking systems in that there is no need for 1/3-party involvement to validate transactions.

Whether you're a Blockchain fanatic or rookie investor, five essential DeFi duties have prolonged-time period funding advantages you may depend on every time and day. These systems moreover have an large impact on each nearby and international economic perspectives.

Overview of Major DeFi Platforms

Ethereum ($ETH)

It is not out of location to mention that Ethereum is the outstanding famous DeFi venture as it office work the underlying blockchain platform for maximum DeFi protocols. The platform gives the Blockchain template upon which many DeFi protocols are constructed and operated. It moreover offers Ethereum's close by token for fee transfer and charge.

The call for for Ethereum and its community token will probably growth due to using DeFi protocols and terrific boom in its panorama. Ethereum is wanted for many things, but ultimately, it's far vital to pay for a gas charge that every client should pay to access DeFi protocols. This brought about ETH tokens being burned and further often than no longer brought on a reduction in the supply of Ether and speedy rate increase.

AAVE ($AAVE)

AAVE is in the long run the most essential multi-chain cash platform wherein customers can borrow or lend hundreds of digital currencies in a non-custodial way. Currently, the marketplace has greater than $6 billion in ordinary fee locked (TVL) and offers many DeFi services collectively with flash loans, excessive-yield financial savings, and tokenized real-world belongings.

Another unique thing about AAVE is that the platform offers close by $AAVE tokens that allow customers to stake their cash to earn 8% APY. AAVE's borrowing and lending protocol is broadly and presently available on numerous networks, together with Polygon, Ethereum, Arbitrum, and so on.

Binance Smart Chain

Binance Chain is regarded because the residence of BNB currencies, and it has grown quicker than anticipated nowadays. This platform guarantees to offer the quickest and maximum reliable decentralized shopping for and promoting. The Binance Smart chain, however, has emerged to come to be a platform that gives a whole-featured decentralized environment constructed at the modern-day day blockchain generation.

After a a success attempt at taking walks the Binance chain in 2020, the platform brought the Binance Smart chain. This platform is derived first of all from Go Ethereum, but, with a few changes to differentiate it from the best Ethereum. Part of the place of distinction is the Proof of Work. At the identical time, the unique Ethereum uses the PoW, and Binance Smart Chain leverages a Proof of Stake Authority consensus mechanism, that is designed to reduce each the time and charge of transactions at the platform.

GMX ($GMX)

GMX is any other multi-chain derivatives market on BNB Chain, Arbitrum, and Avalanche, Arbitrum that lets in customers to alternate futures, perpetual alternatives, and contracts with as much as 25x leverage. Currently, the platform offers over 25 searching for and selling pairs for cryptocurrencies together with Solana,

Cosmos, Bitcoin, Uniswap, and others. Also, the platform has over $4 hundred million in TVL.

This platform emerged as one of the most famous structures in 2023 due to the reality the protocol ratings 0.33 in price-incomes blockchain to be had in the space. The growth in fees is hooked up with the excessive buying and selling quantity on the platform, which results in huge staking rewards in staking for GMX stakes over 30% APY, that is each day fee.

Stargate Finance ($STG)

Stargate Finance ($STG) is every other most relied on waft-chain bridge in the market. It permits clients to switch their assets from one network layer to each other. For example, clients can get entry to their assets from Layer 1 and Layer 2 networks, from either Optimism, Fantom, Ethereum, BNB Chain, Arbitrum, and masses of others. The way customers use the platform is expected to expand in profits as extra L1 & L2 chains arise and the call for for interoperability constantly will increase.

Another aspect approximately this platform is that the token itself has hundreds of utility within the protocol, giving voting and sales rights to as many as viable holders. Also, the token additionally allows the clients to get proper of access to the yielding farming and stake swimming pools and get unrestricted get entry to to liquidity mining opportunities.

In all, STG offers an fantastic investment possibility for truely anybody searching out prolonged-term cost boom on a massive marketplace cap DeFi token.

Uniswap ($UNI)

Currently, Uniswap is the most critical decentralized finance (DeFi) alternate to be had on Polygon, Optimisin, Ethereum, Arbitrum, and unique Layer 2 networks. On this platform, buyers use UNI V3 DEX to trade over $1 billion every day. This is why the platform is one of the most profits-making

DeFi systems. The community has moreover prolonged to combine an NFT Marketplace, which makes it a top competitor to NFT systems like LooksRare and Opensea.

Uniswap makes use of the UNI token, it's an ERC-20 token that lets in clients to get right of entry to a enormous form of DeFi offerings at the platform. UNI tokens may be used to engage in offerings together with liquidity mining, insurance, and governance. More so, the token gives users greater blessings, which consist of voting rights for Uniswap's future route and permits them to percentage income as account holders.

Curve Finance ($CRV)

This platform is taken into consideration one of the systems that offers sturdy investment possibilities in the DeFi marketplace. This is due to the reality Curve Finance is a decentralized trade (DEX) that specializes in stablecoin buying and promoting, this is taken into consideration to be the very wonderful popular addressable market in DeFi. However, one of the critical drawbacks of Curve Finance is its excessive liquidity and espresso slippage.

In-depth Analysis of DeFi Use Cases

Undoubtedly, DeFi stays the critical riding stress of disruption for blockchain technology. Most mainly, it creates higher alternatives to conventional economic practices and moreover gives advanced more recent financial requirements like artificial assets. As the financial panorama passes through this transformative change occasioned with the aid of DeFi, it is immoderate time you find out new possibilities. However, possibilities and possibilities are embedded in the development and innovation of DeFi use times. So, it is a exceptional element to analyze and recognize how to research the scopes and possibilities of DeFi use cases as a way to recognize what you could benefit by means of using way of leveraging the DeFi opportunities.

Now, allow's take a look at the most impactful DeFi use cases.

Derivatives and Synthetic Assets

The first we are able to discover right here is the artificial and derivatives assets. Smart contracts allow clients to create tokenized derivatives, and it has emerge as one of the maximum precise DeFi use instances.

Tokenizing a by-product virtually manner putting the rate of a agreement based totally totally on an underlying set of belongings or financial belongings. This monetary asset works precisely like a traditional safety, consisting of fiat currencies, marketplace indexes, inventory fees, and bonds. However, one element you must word about the tokenization of derivatives is that they may be secondary securities, and their rate isn't always consistent. They can change with the price of the number one securities, collectively with fiat currencies or bonds. This is why we regularly say that they will be essential in growing synthetic property.

Synthetix and dYdX are some of the principle DeFi duties targeted on tokenized derivatives.

Asset Management

One of the excellent advantages that DeFi structures offer their clients is unrestricted get entry to to the manipulate of their bills. Most of those structures permit users to control their belongings, which includes moving virtual assets and buying and promoting assets. With that, clients may also additionally even earn extra hobby from their digital belongings.

Unlike the traditional financial system, DeFi allows clients to keep information privacy, especially the most touchy statistics about them. For conventional financial structures, the usage of a password does now not mean the group would no longer have get proper of get admission to to for your account. But with a few DeFi responsibilities, like Metamask Gnosis Safe, you may enjoy encryption and storing that facts on your private devices. This method you're the best character that has get admission to to for your asset and manages it the way you need. So, asset control is one of the most realistic decentralized finance use cases for account holders.

Decentralized Autonomous Organizations, or DAOs

Think of DAOs due to the fact the counterpart of centralized monetary companies in DeFi. This is why it remains one of the vital strengths of decentralized finance use instances. In the traditional economic machine, centralized economic businesses play a vast role. These companies perform administrative roles with the aid of the use of helping customers manage their middle economic operations, which includes asset manage, governance implementation, and fundraising. That's why the Ethereum blockchain panorama included decentralized corporations to serve a similar cause. However, Decentralized self enough organizations are thru nature decentralized and do now not examine boundaries imposed by using the use of authorities and important governments.

Analytics and Risk Management Tools

Transparency and decentralization helped create a manner to figure out and check big and super quantities of information for the clients. By giving get proper of get entry to to to the ones statistics, customers could make nicely-knowledgeable organisation selections, decide new financial possibilities, and undertake higher threat control techniques.

The Network Effect of Infrastructure Tooling

In the DeFi panorama, the factors internal a tool can interoperate and be a part of. This function is virtually referred to as composability. The format characteristic acts as a center infrastructure development protocol.

Based on that, DeFi projects are continuously protected through what's known as a network effect.

Adhering to CFT and AML Measurements thru the KYT Mechanism

The conventional monetary systems focused on Know-Your-Customer (KYC) protocols. This layout feature, referred to as KYC, uses hints which may be the largest compliance tools for integrating Countering-the-Financing-of-Terrorism (CFT) and Anti-Money Laundering (AML) measurements.

However, one main drawback related to KYC tips is that they regularly contradict DeFi privacy efforts. But in fixing this trouble, DeFi superior a more moderen idea called the Know-Your-Transaction (KYT) mechanism. This mechanism clearly suggests that the decentralized infrastructure may supply interest to transactional behaviors that the platform addresses in place of looking to decide out customers' identities.

Also, KYT solves problems simultaneously by the use of making certain the purchaser's privateness and tracking the actual-time conduct of the transaction. This makes KYT one of the key scopes for decentralized finance use cases.

Besides all of the use times referred to above, people although use DeFi structures for extraordinary use instances, which encompass a method of decentralized alternate, gaming and eSports, margin trading, prediction systems, and saving in competition to inflation.

Chapter 4: Depth Look At Non-Fungible Tokens

In the virtual age, innovation is privy to no bounds, and Non-Fungible Tokens (NFTs) stand at the forefront of this remarkable evolution. The international of NFTs is a charming fusion of technology, artwork, ownership, and creativity. In this bankruptcy, we are capable of skip on an exploratory adventure into the coronary coronary heart of NFTs, dissecting their essence, operation, and impact on our unexpectedly converting virtual landscape. We begin with the fundamental question: What are NFTs, and the way do they art work? These precise virtual tokens, constructed on blockchain technology, revolutionize the concept of ownership and illustration inside the virtual realm. Let's dive in.

What are NFTs?

Non-fungible tokens, regularly NFTs, represent a groundbreaking magnificence of digital assets. Unlike cryptocurrencies which incorporates Bitcoin or Ethereum, which can be fungible and interchangeable one-to-one, NFTs are completely exquisite and irreplaceable. Each NFT possesses a completely unique identification, making it one of a type.

Key Characteristics of NFTS

Non-Fungible: NFTs are characterized with the aid of their non-fungibility, which means that that that they cannot be traded like-for-like. Each NFT is inimitable, making it a virtual collectable or ownership certificate of a selected object.

Ownership and Provenance: NFTs supply transparency to the possession and facts of digital or bodily assets. Blockchain generation information the chain of custody, proving authenticity and beginning.

Digital Assets: NFTs can encapsulate an intensive shape of virtual or bodily gadgets, which incorporates digital artwork, digital actual assets, track, in-project gadgets, and extra. They have unlocked novel opportunities for creators and creditors.

Smart Contracts: NFTs are predominantly constructed on blockchain structures, often leveraging clever contracts to outline their conduct and attributes. These self-executing contracts automate the switch of possession and provide the regulations governing every NFT.

History of NFTs

Before NFTs, proudly owning virtual property existed as early virtual collectables, collectively with virtual buying and selling playing cards and in-hobby gadgets. However, the ones property have been frequently constrained to unique systems and lacked actual possession facts. Let's discover a yr-to-twelve months assessment of approaches a ways NFTs have come.

2012 - The Emergence of Colored Coins

Coloured cash, a concept at the Bitcoin blockchain, allow users to "coloration" unique bitcoins to represent different property. While now not actual NFTs, this laid the foundation for tokenizing actual-international belongings on a blockchain.

2014 - Rare Pepes and Counterparty

The Rare Pepe undertaking, using the Counterparty platform constructed on pinnacle of Bitcoin, brought the idea of unique virtual collectables. Users created and traded unusual Pepe meme playing cards as NFTs.

2017 - CryptoKitties

CryptoKitties, built on the Ethereum blockchain, delivered NFTs into the mainstream. These virtual cats, each with specific attributes, may be bred and traded. The activity have grow to be so well-known that it congested the Ethereum networks.

2017 - ERC-721 Standard

The Ethereum network introduced the ERC-721 large, defining the shape for NFTs. This large allowed developers to create numerous non-fungible tokens, not restricted to digital cats.

2018 - Virtual Real Estate and Art

NFTs multiplied into virtual actual estate with duties like Decentraland and artwork with systems like SuperRare, in which artists should tokenize their paintings as NFTs.

2020 - Beeple's $69 Million Sale

In March 2021, virtual artist Beeple presented an NFT artwork for $69 million at Christie's public sale house. This event made headlines and underscored the developing interest in NFT paintings.

2021 - Widespread Adoption and Controversies

NFTs made headlines with celebrities like Elon Musk and Mark Cuban endorsing or experimenting with them. However, the NFT vicinity moreover faced troubles associated with environmental effect and copyright problems.

2022 - Expansion into Music and Fashion

NFTs extended their attain into the track organization, with artists liberating track and stay usual overall performance tickets as NFTs. Fashion producers like Gucci and comfort watchmakers also experimented with NFTs.

Ongoing Innovation and Expansion

The NFT place continues to comply with new use times, systems, and standards, collectively with the ERC-1155 favored, which allows for every fungible and non-fungible tokens in a unmarried agreement.

How NFTs Work

Non-fungible tokens (NFTs) have emerged as a groundbreaking stress, presenting a extremely-current length to possession, creativity, and the digital financial system. To draw near the essence of NFTs, it is important to apprehend how they feature at their center. In this section, we're able to discover the area of blockchain generation because the bedrock of NFTs, the technique of tokenization that transforms virtual and physical assets into precise, indivisible tokens, and the manner NFTs redefine the concept of possession and provenance within the digital realm.

Blockchain Technology

NFTs are constructed upon blockchain technology, a decentralized and apparent virtual ledger. Blockchain ensures the safety, authenticity, and immutability of NFT transactions. Each NFT is recorded on the blockchain, which acts as a public and tamper-evidence database. Ethereum is the maximum famous blockchain for NFTs, however it is able to moreover exist on different blockchain structures.

Tokenization of Digital Assets

NFTs encompass the tokenization of digital or bodily assets. This method converts those property into precise, indivisible tokens with extraordinary tendencies. For instance, virtual art work, track, digital actual estate, or in-sport objects may be represented as NFTs. The tokenization way assigns a totally unique virtual fingerprint to each asset, making it distinguishable from others.

Ownership and Provenance

One of the key functions of NFTs is the capability to set up ownership and provenance. When you very personal an NFT, the blockchain facts your ownership in a apparent and immutable manner. This approach actually everybody can trace the entire possession history of an NFT, from its creation to the prevailing owner. Provenance is crucial for verifying the authenticity of virtual assets and their ownership information.

Smart Contracts

NFTs are often ruled with the useful resource of clever contracts, self-executing code that automates severa factors of ownership, transfer, and usage. These smart contracts include the recommendations and behaviors of the NFT. For instance, a smart agreement can define how royalties are allocated to the particular author each time the NFT is resold, making sure artists acquire ongoing reimbursement. When a person purchases or transfers an NFT, the smart settlement enforces the ones suggestions and updates ownership at the blockchain.

Uniqueness and Value Proposition of NFTs

Digital Ownership: NFTs supply virtual ownership, permitting human beings to have true possession of digital or digital property. Unlike traditional virtual documents, which can be with out issue duplicated or shared, NFTs offer a unique evidence of possession on the blockchain. This possession extends to virtual property, inclusive of art work, tune, digital actual belongings, and in-sport gadgets.

Scarcity and Rarity: NFTs create digital shortage and rarity. Each NFT is one-of-a-kind or part of a limited series, making it inherently treasured. The idea of shortage drives call for, as creditors are interested in proudly proudly owning some factor particular or uncommon. Artists and creators can use this shortage to growth the desirability and charge in their art work.

Interoperability and Cross-Platform Usage: NFTs are designed to be interoperable, due to this they'll be used throughout high-quality systems and programs. For example, an NFT representing a virtual sword in a exercising must potentially be implemented in multiple video video games that manual NFT integration. This skip-platform compatibility lets in clients to keep their digital belongings from one digital world to a few other, improving their utility and fee.

Benefits of NFTs to Creators and Collectors

NFTs provide numerous benefits to creators and lenders. Creators can:

They can set the terms in their NFTs, along with royalties on secondary profits.

Monetize their work: NFTs provide artists, musicians, and one-of-a-type content cloth creators with new revenue streams, often via selling their digital creations right away to their audience.

Prove authenticity: NFTs can verify the authenticity of digital assets, decreasing the danger of piracy or counterfeiting.

The ERC-721

The ERC-721 cutting-edge, short for "Ethereum Request for Comments 721," is a technical significant at the Ethereum blockchain mainly designed for developing non-fungible tokens (NFTs). The primary function of ERC-721 is the individuality of every token. Each token has a awesome identifier and can't be interchanged with each one of a kind NFT.

Key Features of The ERC-721

Uniqueness: Each token is inherently fantastic and can't be substituted one-to-one, making it best for representing unique digital or bodily property.

Provenance: ERC-721 tokens maintain a obvious and immutable file of ownership and records, making sure authenticity.

Transferability: NFTs conforming to ERC-721 may be securely transferred or traded on numerous marketplaces.

Smart Contracts: Smart contracts outline the behaviors and attributes of every NFT, which include any royalties for creators on secondary income.

Use Cases of the ERC-721

The ERC-721 trendy has decided programs in numerous fields, which incorporates:

Digital Art: Artists use ERC-721 tokens to symbolize their digital artwork as particular collectables.

Gaming: In-game items and characters are tokenized as ERC-721 NFTs, permitting gamers to personal and exchange them.

Collectables: Virtual collectables, consisting of buying and promoting gambling gambling cards and virtual pets, are created as ERC-721 NFTs.

Chapter 5: Nfts In Art, Gaming, And Other Industries

Recently, the art work global has long beyond through giant adjustments with the arrival of Non-fungible tokens. To say that NFT is bringing extraordinary adjustments into the enterprise is an understatement. The fact is, NFT is not doing so in the company, but it is also advancing one of a kind industries with impossible adjustments, reworking the way artwork is offered and supplied.

NFTs are super, one-of-a-type virtual belongings which can represent a few aspect like tune, motion snap shots, or even physical devices. These tokens are saved on the blockchain, making them regular and immutable. As it's far relevant to digital currencies, the blockchain serves because of the fact the digital ledger wherein all transactions are recorded.

The effect of NFTs has been profound within the artwork worldwide. The token has made it less difficult for rookie artwork creators to monetize their creativity. By minting their creativity on the NFT platform, art work creators can sell their paintings creations straight away to any fascinated customers without the want for a intermediary. This gives an open possibility for creators to make coins right away from their creativity.

NFT and Gaming Industry

One of the most important industries which have professional the full-size adjustments that NFTs are bringing on board is the gaming enterprise. In 2021, the worldwide gaming market assessment become anticipated at near $two hundred billion, and it is forecasted to increase at a CAGR of 10.1% from 2021 to 2030. This increase in capability may be related to enhancements in era and a upward thrust in the style of gamers globally.

With this fast boom, but, comes a developing variety of controversies and criticisms. One of the maximum considerably noted stressful conditions is the increase within the microtransactions patterns and pay-to-win in cutting-edge gaming.

More criticisms have been on the character of the game and the sort of game enthusiasts it goals. Notably, the system is criticized for being an exploitative tactic that specializes in gamers who are inclined, especially kids or people who lack impulse manage or conflict with addictive tendencies. Also, it wastes the gamer's money and time, as the ones in-exercise belongings are well actually well worth not anything after purchasing for. But the solution is definitely NFTs. At this juncture, it's far secure to mention that the NFT gaming marketplace stays in its infancy level, even though it is already attracting big interest and funding.

How NFTs are Transforming the Gaming Sector

As anyone may agree with, NFTs are already having a great have an effect on at the gaming organization. While maximum studios haven't begun to combine NFTs, the asset has been applied in making severa gaming programs, together with virtual collectibles and objects, in-pastime skins and gadgets, digital real property, and lands. More so, numerous stores and e-change systems have observed NFTs as part of their services. One corporation we are able to relate to is Nike. This organization has patented its CryptoKicks.

Ways NFTs are Revolutionizing the Art World

Ownership and Authenticating of creations

With NFTs, art work creators can bid farewell to moments of art work forgery within the business enterprise. NFT solves the long-status trouble of paintings forgery by way of using making sure each art work is traceable to a particular deliver or owner. This technique each NFT is precise and can not be replicated or altered through using the use of anybody everywhere. This lets in to make sure proof of possession and authenticity of a piece.

NFT is backed via way of a blockchain that allows creators to mint their artwork onto it, designing a digital certificates of a chunk that follows an artwork to wherever it is bought or offered. This gadget allows to guarantee receive as real with and transparency in the art work market. It moreover curbs highbrow theft amongst creators.

Pushing the frontiers of art work

Many creators could not have imagined a time might in all likelihood come whilst their creativity is probably digitalized and celebrated. They possibly ought to have believed the best terrain wherein their creativity is probably brilliant valued is the bodily worldwide. With the appearance of NFT, it is the dawn of a brand new generation and opportunities. Now, we are capable to speak approximately paintings and talk approximately digitalization. Virtual sculptures can now be digitalized and bought at greater valuable expenses than they changed into bodily.

Creating new sales approach and royalty schemes for creators

Unlike the antique machine wherein arts are constrained to the bodily global and may handiest be monetized through which means, creators now have the opportunity to monetize their art work via earning royalties anyplace their work is bought, imparting a sustainable method of earning. For creators, NFT is one of the dependable procedures to earn passively.

Democratizing art work collection and enhancing participation

Formerly, the paintings international became a domain for the elite. Only the ones who have the property can discover the market. But now, the appearance of NFT has introduced about a first-rate trade, so much definitely so with your system connected to the internet, you can turn out to be an artwork creator and earn as an lousy lot as possible. These contents may be supplied, created, and bought, thereby developing a decentralized marketplace that encourages wider involvement.

Digital accessibility breaks down region obstacles, permitting art fans to engage globally in what they love and make coins on the same time as doing so. NFTs are democratizing the marketplace through supplying access to worldwide systems in which artists and creditors will have interaction proper now, removing the want for middlemen or organizations, collectively with public sale houses or galleries.

Promoting precise interaction with paintings

NFTs aren't pretty lots how we buy and sell paintings collectibles; they are moreover converting how we have interaction with the ones gadgets. Some collectibles are attractive and interactive, permitting art creators to alter the art work and engage with it uniquely.

How Gaming Is Adopting NFTs For In-Game Assets

Playing video games gives you a completely unique and remarkable experience that you could have even as wearing out specific types of media. However, the developing gaming device is based carefully on centralized systems, giving precise platform manipulate to corporations interior the game. This shape made it possible for gamers to purchase gaming NFTs, similarly to supply greater income to those gaming organizations. Gaming companies which have incorporated this opportunity are Ubisoft, Epic Games, EA, Nintendo, and others.

Other Innovative Applications of NFTs in Various Industries

NFT isn't most effective bringing modern modifications to the economic and artwork worlds; the generation is also appearing as a transformative stress, changing the way unique industries characteristic and supply their offerings.

Fashion Industry: one of the industries exploring the ability of NFTs is the fashion location. The fashion corporation leverages NFTs to create virtual representations of fashion items such as digital avatars, accessories, and apparel. This lets in fashion manufacturers to promote unique, present day day-model digital style devices, developing some different way of getting cash for designers. In special terms, NFTs create a modern-day device for designers to monetize their creativity and engage with customers. In addition, NFTs can provide proof of possession and authenticity for style gadgets, thereby supporting restrict the chance of fake or counterfeiting.

Chapter 6: The Economics Of Defi And Nfts

In current years, finance and era have witnessed a transformative evolution driven through manner of groundbreaking upgrades—Decentralized Finance (DeFi) and Non-Fungible Tokens (NFTs). DeFi, with its basis on blockchain technology, has ushered in a new technology of decentralized and without borders monetary offerings, tough traditional intermediaries and redefining how people' get right of entry to, manipulate, and invest their assets. Simultaneously, NFTs have unleashed a revolution in the digital and modern geographical regions, presenting artists, content material material creators, and collectors with current gear to tokenize and change precise digital property. The synergy among DeFi and NFTs paperwork a dynamic stress reshaping now not handiest the monetary landscape but additionally the very thoughts of finance and possession. This financial ruin will find out the shifts added about through the ones virtual phenomena and their profound implications for traditional finance.

The Principle of DeFi

DeFi, quick for Decentralized Finance, is a progressive concept that leverages blockchain generation to create an open, obvious, decentralized economic environment. At its center, DeFi is constructed upon numerous key principles that set it other than traditional finance. Below are some of these standards

Decentralization: One of the important ideas of DeFi is the removal of centralized intermediaries like banks and economic institutions. Instead, financial transactions arise immediately among friends on blockchain networks. This decentralization reduces the want for accept as authentic with in 0.33 occasions and fosters financial inclusivity.

Open and Permissionless: DeFi systems are open to anybody with a web connection and a well suited pockets. There are not any eligibility standards or gatekeepers, making those financial services handy to a global audience. It's a without boundary lines and inclusive gadget that worrying conditions the exclusivity of conventional finance.

Smart Contracts: DeFi is primarily based intently on clever contracts, which can be self-executing contracts with the terms of the settlement right away written into code. These contracts automate severa monetary processes, from lending and borrowing to shopping for and selling and asset manipulate. They are open deliver and apparent, permitting trustless transactions.

Transparency: DeFi transactions and clever contracts are recorded on public blockchains, making all sports sports visible to everyone. This transparency complements receive as real with and protection, as customers can verify transactions and contracts independently, decreasing the hazard of fraud or manipulation.

Interoperability: DeFi projects are frequently designed to art work together, allowing customers to get admission to severa monetary offerings in the environment. This interoperability creates a dynamic and interconnected community wherein belongings can glide seamlessly among superb packages.

Tokenization: DeFi tokens constitute diverse assets, which incorporates cryptocurrencies, actual-international assets, and different financial gadgets. Tokenization allows for fractional possession, multiplied liquidity, and the introduction of particular financial products. These tokens can be traded, lent, borrowed, and staked in diverse DeFi protocols.

Cryptocurrency in DeFi

Cryptocurrencies play a significant characteristic in DeFi (Decentralized finance), serving because of the fact the number one medium of change and the muse of many

DeFi packages. Here are some key factors of the position of cryptocurrencies in DeFi:

Medium of Exchange: Cryptocurrencies like Ethereum (ETH), Bitcoin (BTC), and stablecoins which includes DAI and USDC are usually used due to the fact the number one medium of change in DeFi. Users want those virtual property to participate in DeFi sports activities sports, consisting of shopping for and selling, lending, and borrowing.

Collateral: Cryptocurrencies regularly characteristic collateral in DeFi lending and borrowing structures. Users can lock up their crypto holdings as collateral to gain loans in stablecoins or considered one of a kind cryptocurrencies. This collateralization lets in customers to get right of access to liquidity without selling their crypto belongings.

Liquidity: Cryptocurrencies provide liquidity for decentralized exchanges and lending structures. Liquidity vendors make a contribution cryptocurrencies to liquidity swimming pools in pass lower lower back for charges and rewards, facilitating buying and promoting and lending sports activities inside the DeFi surroundings.

Governance Tokens: Many DeFi systems trouble governance tokens to customers who offer liquidity or take part in platform activities. These tokens, regularly based totally on cryptocurrencies, supply holders the electricity to vote on platform enhancements, modifications, and hints.

Yield Farming and Staking: Cryptocurrencies actively participate in yield farming and staking techniques interior DeFi. Users can stake their crypto property or offer liquidity to earn rewards through more cryptocurrencies, inclusive of governance tokens.

Payment for Services: In DeFi, cryptocurrencies pay various services and charges, together with transaction fees, gasoline prices on Ethereum, and prices for interacting with DeFi protocols. Users need to maintain cryptocurrencies to pay for the ones offerings.

NFTs and their Uniqueness

NFTs are virtual tokens representing ownership or proof of authenticity of a totally unique object or content fabric on a blockchain. Unlike cryptocurrencies which includes Bitcoin or Ethereum, NFTs aren't interchangeable due to the reality every is outstanding. NFTs derive their rate from the fact that they may be one-of-a-kind or a part of a restricted version. This place of knowledge is frequently linked to virtual paintings, collectibles, and awesome scarce digital property. NFTs moreover offer smooth possession and provenance of virtual content material, because the blockchain records the whole information of the NFT, making it tough to counterfeit or duplicate.

Use Cases for NFTs

Art: NFTs have revolutionized the art work global by using manner of allowing artists to tokenize their virtual creations. Buyers collect possession and provenance of digital works of art, and artists can earn royalties on secondary profits.

Gaming: NFTs are implemented in video video games to symbolize in-endeavor assets, characters, and skins. Gamers can purchase, sell, and trade the ones digital gadgets on NFT marketplaces.

Collectibles: NFTs have breathed new existence into virtual collectibles, which includes trading playing gambling playing cards and digital objects. Collectors can show possession and rarity, and marketplaces allow shopping for and selling.

Virtual Real Estate: In virtual worlds like Decentraland and The Sandbox, NFTs represent parcels of digital land. Owners can expand, promote, or rent their virtual houses.

Music and Entertainment: Musicians, celebrities, and content creators use NFTs to release specific content material cloth, live performance tickets, and merchandise. NFTs offer a right away revenue circulate and fan engagement.

Potential Long-Term Impacts On Traditional Finance

The rise of DeFi (Decentralized Finance) and NFTs (Non-Fungible Tokens) has the functionality to carry great and lasting impacts to standard finance. One of the essential disruptions lies within the principle of disintermediation that DeFi embraces. As DeFi structures take away the want for conventional monetary intermediaries together with banks, the position and function an effect on of those establishments in the financial tool may additionally step by step reduce. Over time, this shift should reason a redefinition of the traditional banking version as extra clients turn to decentralized alternatives for lending, borrowing, and other economic services.

Chapter 7: Security, Regulation, And Ethical Considerations

It is not data that Decentralized finance (DeFi) offers a paradigm shift in the financial panorama, particularly because it offers customers get right of get entry to to to borrow cryptocurrencies using their assets as collateral or lend out virtual currencies for earnings. However, as with every nascent generation, DeFi is confronted with a difficult and speedy of protection, law, and moral challenges that each one stakeholders concerned have to thoroughly look at and cope with.

In recent years, DeFi structures and protocols have confronted numerous breaches and hacks that compromised their safety good sized and prompted massive monetary losses for his or her users. The majority of the breaches and attacks have been the final outcomes of DeFi protection worrying situations associated with rug pulls, smart settlement vulnerabilities, lack of installed regulatory frameworks, oracle manipulations, heavy reliance on some centralized components, and common and simple human mistakes.

Like every distinctive software program application framework, DeFi apps are liable to exploits and hacks. Hackers can use flaws in DeFi apps to manipulate transactions or steal coins. Exploits and hacks can purpose considerable monetary losses and damage the recognition of DeFi systems or apps.

Most instances, DeFi protection issues are determined because of protection flaws in clever contracts. As you have got were given have a look at, smart contracts function the foundation of DeFi apps, allowing financial transactions to take vicinity robotically. These clever contracts are liable to mistakes, bugs, and different vulnerabilities that hackers can make the maximum. This is why specialists often warn that everybody have to be careful approximately clever contracts' flaws. One number one truth approximately clever contracts flaws is they often bring about loss of rate range because of the reality attackers can modify the code to steal cash or motive financial disruption.

DeFi Regulatory Challenge

Another largest challenge going through DeFi is regulatory uncertainty. To date, DeFi regulatory readability remains a huge problem for each developers and clients. More so, many countries are however to pitch their tent with DeFi because of the fact there may be no route as regards litigation. While some nations have been substantially friendly to DeFi, maximum famous ones are despite the fact that extra sceptical. But one unsure factor is how DeFi systems is probably regulated inside the destiny. This is developing a nightmare and uncertainty for each DeFi customers and builders, as they'll not recognize a way to stay inside the confines of the law.

As DeFi keeps to grow, regulators around the region are paying near interest. This three hundred and sixty five days, we might also welcome more regulatory clarity round DeFi. However, regulators will need to obtain a compromise, in particular to do with setting a balance among promoting innovation and protecting clients. This regulatory readability is more than essential because it permits to power the prolonged-term boom of the phenomenon inside the DeFi surroundings.

More so, it's miles vital to u . S . That virtual protection lapses don't handiest have an effect on DeFi but furthermore NFTs. The truth that each are built on the identical Blockchain generation, they may be at risk of the same or comparable protection stressful conditions. However, common NFT cybercrimes are phishing emails, rug-pull scams, pump-and-sell off schemes, identification fraud, and faux tokens.

NFTs have brought about cyber protection and also many fraudulent instances. With the increase of this new era, black-hat hackers have positioned a manner to benefit a bonus of the system. Many hackers normally have a tendency to create non-present stores with the potential to mirror the logo and contents of the particular NFT hold. These faux NFTs can be took place as the unique issue and purchased at an high priced cost, essential to a person searching for a fake NFT, which often results in copyright issues for the motive that there can best be one NFT with the equal capabilities.

Addressing the Security Challenges in DeFi and NFTs

It is clearer now than ever that navigating the DeFi and NFT universes without sturdy safety capabilities is hooked up to crusing turbulent waters without a compass that could help cope with the hassle. Since we've discussed numerous traumatic situations related to those important figures within the virtual location, it's miles pretty important we take a step further to have a study possible techniques the ones problems may be resolved in order that every developers and customers can enjoy the opportunities that every structures offer.

NFT solutions are -fold - one is for NFT creators and protocol owners. Then, the second is designed for the customers. For the protocol owners, the primary answer is for them to prioritize audits. If you have got have a look at appreciably about NFT protection, you may agree that audits are the power that gives robust help for NFT cyber protection. Audits make certain all loopholes are well closed simply so codes aren't exploited.

Another solution is to undertake decentralized garage for metadata. The maximum crucial art work of metadata is to shield the distinctiveness of NFTs and ensure they may be now not inclined. More

so, developers need to make certain to stick through to clever settlement excellent practices. Also, developers need to make certain the practices are carried out as clearly and with out problems as possible.

However, for the users, pockets safety may be very important and want to be held within the most regard. Users should be allowed to adopt the three-Wallet method and embody greater pockets hints to ensure steady transactions at the NFT platform.

Ethical Considerations and The Environmental Impact Of Blockchain Technology

We have noted why and the way blockchain generation has been hailed because the transformative force within the financial business enterprise. However, this generation comes with some moral troubles and environmental affects we need to not forget.

The first moral trap 22 scenario of blockchain technology is privateness and records safety. Though this era is often portrayed as a non-public and consistent manner of making transactions, the query of private records control and capacity misuse through a few people is an hassle that can be swept below the carpet.

The 2nd dilemma is accessibility and equity. Blockchain's high electricity necessities can enlarge gift inequalities. This will vicinity accessibility simplest within the hands of those who can control to pay for the energy value and extraordinary vital device, leaving people without get proper of access to inside the again of and growing a virtual divide.

The 0.33 ethical hobby is hacking and cybercrime. DeFi requires a government for governance, posing a top notch moral assignment. Such generation might be used for nefarious capabilities, which incorporates terrorism financing and cash laundering.

Mitigating Environmental Impact

Besides some of the moral issues surrounding the usage of blockchain era cited above, every other problem we can't chide away from is the environmental effect it creates being an strength-huge gadget.

Chapter 8: The Future Of Defi And Nfts

The future of NFTs and DeFi gives promising avenues of innovation and disruption in the economic and digital asset landscapes. These groundbreaking technology are on the cusp of redefining how we've got interplay with assets, financial offerings, and virtual ownership. In this bankruptcy, we can delve into the exciting trends shaping the route earlier, exploring the convergence of DeFi and NFTs, the growth of decentralized finance to embody actual-global belongings, and the profound effect these trends may additionally have on the financial enterprise. Let's dive in.

Emerging Trends in DeFi and NFTs

The international of DeFi (Decentralized Finance) and NFTs (Non-Fungible Tokens) is in a regular kingdom of evolution, with developing tendencies shaping the destiny of those groundbreaking generation. As blockchain ecosystems increase and mature, new opportunities emerge that promise to disrupt traditional monetary systems and redefine the idea of digital ownership. In this section, we find out the dynamic and ever-converting landscape of DeFi and NFTs, losing moderate at the contemporary-day inclinations reshaping the ones technology.

DeFi for Real-World Assets: DeFi is expanding past cryptocurrencies to tokenize actual-worldwide property along side actual property, artwork, and shares. The capability to invest in the ones belongings with fractional possession will preserve developing, in all likelihood reworking traditional asset commands.

Layer 2 Scaling Solutions: To cope with scalability and immoderate gas fees, DeFi responsibilities are actively exploring Layer 2 scaling solutions. These solutions intention to beautify the performance and rate-effectiveness of DeFi transactions at the same time as retaining security.

NFT Utility and Interoperability: NFTs are evolving past collectibles and paintings. They are incorporated into numerous applications, along with virtual worlds, gaming, and training. The interoperability of NFTs all through outstanding systems is a promising development.

Decentralized Identity and Reputation Systems: DeFi and NFTs are paving the way for decentralized identification and recognition structures. Users can leverage their blockchain-primarily based completely simply credentials and records for various features, from borrowing to gaining access to incredible content cloth material.

The Future of DeFi and NFTs Integration with Traditional Finance

Integrating DeFi (Decentralized Finance) and NFTs (Non-Fungible Tokens) with conventional finance heralds a modern-day generation within the financial panorama. This merging of contemporary blockchain technology with the established structures of conventional finance opens a worldwide of possibilities and challenges. In this segment, we are able to find out the dynamic panorama wherein those worlds meet and the way this integration is reshaping the future of finance.

Hybrid Finance: The destiny also can witness a fusion of DeFi and conventional finance. Established financial institutions are exploring possibilities to mix DeFi services into their services, allowing users to get proper of get entry to to the outstanding of every worlds.

Regulatory Adaptation: As DeFi and NFTs develop, regulatory frameworks will adapt. Traditional finance will an increasing number of coexist with decentralized finance, necessitating clear regulatory guidelines to make sure user safety and safety.

Mainstream Adoption: DeFi and NFTs may additionally need to accumulate massive mainstream adoption. More human beings and companies will apprehend the benefits of decentralized monetary services and precise virtual ownership, reshaping how we've got interaction with belongings and monetary products.

Asset Tokenization: The tokenization of actual-world belongings will enlarge, potentially main to a revolution in how conventional property like actual assets and shares are controlled, traded, and invested in.

Digital Identity and Financial Inclusion: Integrating DeFi and NFTs into conventional finance should enhance virtual identity structures and sell economic inclusion as people worldwide get admission to severa financial offerings.

Preparing for a Decentralized Future

Preparing for the decentralized destiny is important as DeFi (Decentralized Finance) and NFTs (Non-Fungible Tokens) hold to reshape the monetary landscape. Here's what readers want to recognize as they navigate this evolving surroundings:

Stay well-knowledgeable and informed: To put together for the decentralized destiny, readers should make investments time knowledge the fundamentals of blockchain generation, DeFi, and NFTs. Being nicely-knowledgeable is step one in making sound choices in this rapidly converting vicinity.

Risk Assessment: DeFi and NFTs provide good sized possibilities, however in addition they encompass particular dangers, which encompass clever agreement vulnerabilities, marketplace volatility, and regulatory uncertainties. Readers should cautiously take a look at and control those risks.

Diversification is fundamental: Diversifying one's portfolio is a key technique. Rather than setting all belongings proper right into a unmarried DeFi undertaking or NFT collection, bear in mind spreading investments during one-of-a-kind assets and structures to mitigate threat.

Regulatory Compliance: Stay knowledgeable approximately the evolving regulatory landscape surrounding DeFi and NFTs. Different international places also can have various techniques, so it is vital to conform with neighborhood hints to keep away from criminal problems.

DeFi Staking and Yield Farming: If undertaking DeFi sports like staking or yield farming, understand the associated dangers and rewards. Make knowledgeable picks based totally definitely completely on the platform's protection and the property concerned.

Long-Term Perspective: DeFi and NFTs are however in their early levels, and the space is rapidly evolving. Readers need to undertake an extended-time period attitude, as a few obligations might also take time to mature and monitor their right capability.

User Experience: Evaluate the character experience of DeFi structures and NFT marketplaces. User-great interfaces and easy instructions are critical for easy interactions in this decentralized global.

Chapter 9: The Rise Of Nfts

NFTs represent a paradigm shift inside the way we recognize possession and charge within the virtual realm. Unlike crypto currencies together with Bit coin or Ethereum which is probably fungible (which means every unit is interchangeable), NFTs are indivisible and specific. Each token holds wonderful trends that set it aside from every different.

The idea of NFTs may be traced decrease again to the early days of block chain generation when builders sought techniques to tokenize assets beyond traditional currencies. However, it wasn't until 2017 with the discharge of Crypto Kitties on the Ethereal block chain that NFTs won great popularity.

Crypto Kitties allowed customers to acquire, breed, purchase, and promote virtual cats the use of Ether (ETH). Each cat becomes represented with the useful useful resource of an character token on the block chain with its very non-public set of attributes like color, pattern, and rarity. This easy but present day concept sparked hobby amongst tech-savvy those who found capacity for utilizing this idea beyond virtual pets.

As hobby grew round Crypto Kitties' success tale, artists commenced exploring how they will leverage this generation to create particular digital artistic endeavors. They positioned out that via minting their creations as NFTs on block chains like Ethereal or Binance Smart Chain (BSC), they may installation verifiable ownership at the same time as preserving scarcity in a digital medium.

The art work worldwide short embraced this new form of expression as creators positioned freedom in bypassing conventional gatekeepers collectively with galleries or auction houses. With just a few clicks, artists may also want to now achieve international audiences without delay through on-line marketplaces dedicated to shopping for and promoting NFT paintings.

One key difficulty that contributed to the rise of NFTs emerge as the functionality to show authenticity and possession via blockchain era. The decentralized nature of blockchains ensures transparency, immutability, and traceability, doing away with issues about counterfeit or stolen digital artwork.

Moreover, NFTs provided a way to the prolonged-status venture of monetizing virtual content. Artists who previously struggled to earn a dwelling from their online creations now had an street for promoting their art work proper away to lenders. This newfound monetary empowerment attracted artists from diverse disciplines - painters, musicians, photographers, or maybe meme creators - all eager to discover this thrilling frontier.

The mainstream media started out taking be conscious as nicely whilst immoderate-profile income made headlines throughout the arena. Beeple's artwork "Everydays: The First 5000 Days" presented for a first rate $69 million at auction in March 2021, solidifying NFTs' location in well-known subculture.

As greater artists embraced NFTs and greater creditors joined the movement, marketplaces devoted absolutely to buying and promoting these unique tokens started doping up like mushrooms after rain. Platforms at the side of OpenSea, Rarible, SuperRare have come to be hubs wherein buyers can also moreover need to find out new creative endeavors even as supporting their preferred creators.

However, it's far important now not to overlook the criticisms surrounding NFTs. Concerns about environmental impact due to electricity-enormous blockchain mining strategies have been raised thru activists and experts alike. Additionally, questions regarding copyright infringement and highbrow assets rights indoors this nascent enterprise need cautious interest transferring beforehand.

Despite those traumatic situations and debates surrounding NFTs' destiny trajectory stays unsure; one element is plain: they have got undeniably disrupted conventional notions of artwork possession and spread out new possibilities for each creators and lenders in our increasingly more digitized international.

In next chapters of this e book we are capable of delve deeper into understanding non-fungible tokens (NFTs), exploring their origins,

how they may be created using blockchain generation,

their effect on artwork markets,

the prison concerns surrounding NFT possession,

and the capability future packages of this groundbreaking technology. So, fasten your seatbelts as we embark on an interesting journey into the vicinity of NFTs!

Understanding Non-Fungible Tokens (NFTs)

In this economic ruin, we're capable of delve into the concept of non-fungible tokens

(NFTs) and discover their precise tendencies that set them other than traditional cryptocurrencies. NFTs have won super attention in modern-day years, revolutionizing the way we understand and engage with virtual property.

To recognize NFTs, it's miles important to recognise the perception of fungibility. Unlike fungible assets which incorporates cryptocurrencies or fiat currencies, which is probably interchangeable on a one-to-one foundation, NFTs very own first-rate homes that make every token precise and irreplaceable.

One key detail of NFTs is their indivisibility. While cryptocurrencies can be divided into smaller gadgets like satoshis or wei, NFTs can not be damaged down into smaller fractions without losing their inherent charge. Each NFT represents an entire entity or object in preference to a divisible unit.

Furthermore, a few other defining characteristic of NFTs is their immutability.

Once an asset is tokenized as an NFT on a blockchain community, its ownership records and metadata grow to be genuinely recorded on the allotted ledger. This transparency guarantees authenticity and prevents fraudulent sports sports associated with counterfeit virtual property.

Additionally, in contrast to traditional creative endeavors or collectibles that require bodily presence for verification purposes, NFT possession can be without trouble proven thru blockchain technology. The decentralized nature of blockchains gets rid of the want for intermediaries thru supplying obvious evidence of possession immediately on the public ledger.

Moreover, creators have the capability to embed specific attributes within an NFT's clever agreement code. These attributes can encompass facts about provenance, scarcity levels, royalties for future resales, or even interactive functions that allow owners to have interaction with their virtual belongings in particular processes.

The market for NTF art work has skilled exponential increase in contemporary years because of its capability for artists to monetize their paintings right now with out depending entirely on galleries or public sale homes. Artists now have the possibility to gain a worldwide purpose marketplace and accumulate without delay bills for his or her creations.

However, it is vital to notice that NFTs extend past the location of artwork. They have determined packages in numerous industries which incorporates gaming, music, style, or perhaps real belongings. The versatility of NFTs allows for countless opportunities in phrases of tokenizing digital or bodily assets.

As we maintain our exploration into the arena of NFTs, it turns into glaring that those tokens represent a paradigm shift in how we understand ownership and fee in the virtual age. With their particular homes and capability use times in the path of multiple sectors, NFTs are poised to reshape industries and redefine our data of virtual assets.

In the following economic disaster, we will delve deeper into the origins of NFTs and discover how this groundbreaking generation got here into lifestyles. Stay tuned as we find the fascinating data at the back of non-fungible tokens!

Exploring the Origins of NFTs

In order to certainly apprehend the significance and effect of Non-Fungible Tokens (NFTs), it is important to delve into their origins. The concept of NFTs may be traced over again to the early days of blockchain era, in which developers sought to create a very unique virtual asset that couldn't be replicated or counterfeited.

The start of NFTs may be attributed to the desire for authenticity and shortage within the digital realm. Prior to their existence, digital documents had been consequences copied and shared without any distinction amongst real and duplicate variations. This posed a mission for artists, creators, and creditors who preferred a manner to installation ownership and fee within the an increasing number of digitized international.

It changed into in 2012 whilst Colored Coins emerged as one of the earliest tries at tokenizing property on pinnacle of Bitcoin's blockchain. While now not especially designed for art work or collectibles, this innovation laid a few foundation for what could later end up NFTs. However, it wasn't until Ethereum got here onto the scene with its clever agreement capabilities that real non-fungibility have turn out to be possible.

Ethereum's advent in 2015 revolutionized blockchain technology through permitting builders to create programmable contracts called clever contracts. These contracts enabled people to outline rules and situations spherical ownership, transferability, royalties, and greater inner a decentralized network.

One terrific project that executed an instrumental function in shaping NFTs changed into CryptoPunks. Launched through Larva Labs in 2017 as an test on Ethereum's blockchain, CryptoPunks brought unique pixelated characters with tremendous attributes together with hairstyles, accessories, and backgrounds. Each individual have become represented by the use of the usage of an ERC-721 token - one of the first implementations of non-fungible tokens.

CryptoKitties followed fast after in overdue 2017 - any other groundbreaking venture constructed on Ethereum's platform. It allowed clients to breed and trade virtual cats, each represented thru an NFT. The recreation's popularity skyrocketed, inflicting congestion on the Ethereum network and highlighting both the ability and demanding conditions of NFTs.

Chapter 10: How Nfts Are Created And Verified

In this economic damage, we're capable of delve into the tough method of creating and verifying Non-Fungible Tokens (NFTs). NFTs have received large popularity in trendy years because of their particular homes and potential to symbolize possession of digital belongings. Understanding how these tokens are created and validated is vital for everyone interested by exploring the area of NFTs.

To create an NFT, one need to first pick out a blockchain platform that allows the advent of those tokens. Ethereum is currently the most extensively used blockchain for NFTs, way to its strong clever settlement talents. Other blockchains like Binance Smart Chain and Flow moreover offer assist for NFT advent.

Once a suitable blockchain platform is selected, artists or creators can hold with minting their paintings or digital asset as an NFT. Minting refers to the approach of tokenizing a very precise piece of content material material material on the blockchain. This entails attaching metadata collectively with title, description, photograph/video file, and special applicable data to the token.

The verification approach ensures that every newly minted token adheres to precise necessities set through way of the selected blockchain platform. These requirements normally embody compliance with ERC-721 or ERC-1155 protocols on Ethereum-based completely systems. Verification allows hold consistency all through all NFTs internal a specific environment.

After minting and verification, the newly created NFT is assigned a totally unique identifier known as a token ID. This ID distinguishes it from different tokens within the same series or collection. The token ID serves as evidence of authenticity and place of know-how for every body item represented with the resource of the usage of an NFT.

To similarly decorate trustworthiness and transparency in verifying possession rights, many marketplaces put into effect decentralized identifiers (DIDs) linked to clients' wallets. DIDs offer cryptographic evidence that people very personal precise addresses related to their wallets.

Verifying ownership regularly includes interacting with smart contracts deployed on the chosen blockchain network. These clever contracts comprise the common sense and rules governing the switch of possession, royalties, and other components associated with NFT transactions. By executing unique capabilities inner the ones clever contracts, customers can validate their ownership rights.

It's critical to be aware that on the equal time as blockchain technology guarantees immutability and transparency in verifying NFTs, it does no longer assure the fine or price of the underlying virtual asset. Buyers should behavior thorough research earlier than shopping an NFT to make certain its authenticity and desirability.

In precis, growing and verifying NFTs is composed of selecting a suitable blockchain platform, minting the virtual asset as an NFT with accompanying metadata, adhering to verification necessities set thru the chosen platform, assigning a totally unique token ID for every token, imposing decentralized identifiers (DIDs) for client wallets' affiliation with ownership rights, and interacting with clever contracts for validation skills. Understanding this manner is crucial for every creators and customers in navigating the world of Non-Fungible Tokens.

The Backbone of NFTs - Blockchain Technology

Blockchain era performs a pivotal function inside the international of Non-Fungible Tokens (NFTs). It serves because the underlying infrastructure that ensures transparency, safety, and immutability internal this digital environment. Understanding how blockchain abilties is vital to comprehending the real fee and potential of NFTs.

At its center, blockchain is a decentralized ledger that information transactions at some stage in multiple laptop systems or nodes. Each transaction is bundled proper right into a block, it without a doubt is then delivered to a chain of preceding blocks, forming an unalterable file. This allotted nature receives rid of the need for intermediaries and critical authorities, making it pretty evidence against fraud or manipulation.

In relation to NFTs, blockchain acts as a digital certificates of authenticity. By leveraging cryptographic algorithms and clever contracts, every specific token can be securely demonstrated and traced once more to its unique creator or owner. This provides artists with evidence of ownership and establishes provenance for his or her virtual artistic endeavors.

One key function of blockchain era that complements the fee proposition of NFTs is decentralization. Unlike conventional art markets in which gatekeepers control access and distribution channels, blockchain-based systems empower artists via allowing them direct interaction with lenders worldwide. This democratized method fosters inclusivity on the equal time as reducing obstacles to access for growing abilties.

Moreover, blockchain's apparent nature allows real-time tracking of transactions on public ledgers inclusive of Ethereum or Binance Smart Chain. Anyone can view the data of possession transfers associated with an NFT, making sure obligation at some stage in its lifecycle. This degree of transparency instills receive as genuine with among clients who can verify the legitimacy and strong factor before making any buy.

Another advantage furnished with the aid of the usage of blockchain generation in terms of NFTs is fractional ownership. Through tokenization on blockchains like Ethereum the use of ERC-20 necessities or different properly matched protocols like Flow or Tezos; excessive-fee belongings which encompass real assets homes or uncommon collectibles can be divided into smaller fractions represented via NFTs. This opens up new funding opportunities, allowing individuals to very very personal a fraction of an asset that changed into formerly inaccessible.

Furthermore, blockchain technology offers a robust and green market for buying, promoting, and buying and promoting NFTs. Smart contracts automate the execution of transactions, disposing of the need for intermediaries and decreasing transaction expenses. Additionally, blockchain's immutability guarantees that when an NFT is minted or transferred, it can't be altered or tampered with.

As blockchain generation keeps to adapt and scale, so does its effect on the world of NFTs. Layer 2 solutions like Polygon or Optimism are being advanced to deal with scalability issues related to excessive gasoline costs on

Ethereum. These upgrades will permit faster and greater rate-effective transactions whilst retaining the safety furnished through the underlying blockchain infrastructure.

In cease, blockchain era serves because the spine of NFTs thru supplying transparency, protection, decentralization, fractional possession abilities; all even as facilitating seamless transactions inner a international marketplace. Its immutable nature ensures don't forget in provenance and authenticity on the equal time as empowering artists and lenders alike. As we delve deeper into this new era of digital artwork and property ownership thru NFTs; records how blockchain permits these improvements turns into essential for all of us looking for to navigate this exciting landscape correctly.

The Impact of NFTs on Digital Art Marketplaces

The emergence of Non-Fungible Tokens (NFTs) has delivered approximately a massive transformation inside the world of digital paintings marketplaces. These precise tokens, built on blockchain generation, have revolutionized the way artists create, promote, and distribute their art work.

One of the key influences of NFTs on virtual artwork marketplaces is the democratization of get proper of get admission to to. Traditionally, artists had to depend upon galleries or entrepreneurs to showcase and sell their artwork. This often created boundaries for growing artists who struggled to advantage reputation and exposure. However, with NFTs, artists can right now hook up with collectors and customers from everywhere inside the global via decentralized systems.

Moreover, NFTs have added a new degree of transparency within the paintings market. Each token represents a particular piece of paintings and includes embedded information about its provenance and ownership statistics. This gets rid of issues concerning counterfeit or unauthorized reproductions as each transaction is recorded at the blockchain for all of us to peer.

Additionally, NFTs have spread out new sales streams for artists thru royalties from resales. Unlike traditional artwork income in which artists get keep of rate only as quickly as upon initial sale, NFT clever contracts permit creators to earn a percentage whenever their paintings is bought once more in secondary markets. This offers ongoing financial aid for artists even after their preliminary art work has been offered.

Furthermore, NFTs have sparked renewed interest in virtual art work as an funding asset elegance. Collectors in the meanwhile are actively looking for uncommon and valuable virtual artistic endeavors that hold functionality for destiny appreciation in charge. This has introduced about an boom in name for for restrained version quantities thru renowned virtual artists.

With this surge in call for comes extended visibility for each mounted and developing skills within the virtual artwork network. Artists who have been previously left out via traditional institutions now have opportunities to benefit reputation based absolutely on the benefit in their artwork in choice to relying completely on gatekeepers' approval.

However, the rise of NFTs has moreover raised issues approximately sustainability and environmental effect. The electricity intake related to blockchain technology, mainly in evidence-of-artwork systems, has drawn complaint due to its carbon footprint. As the recognition of NFTs keeps to develop, it's miles important for artists and systems to discover greater sustainable alternatives which include transitioning within the path of green blockchains or the use of evidence-of-stake mechanisms.

In surrender, NFTs have had a profound effect on digital art work marketplaces via manner of democratizing get proper of access to, growing transparency, growing new sales streams for artists, and elevating the popularity of virtual paintings as an funding asset magnificence. While there are demanding situations that need to be addressed regarding sustainability, the general have an impact on of NFTs at the artwork global cannot be denied. It is an exciting time for every artists and creditors as they navigate this new generation of virtual possession and creativity.

Collecting and Investing in NFT Artworks

Collecting and making an funding in NFT artistic endeavors has end up a well-known fashion in trendy years. The specific nature of non-fungible tokens gives creditors the possibility to personal digital assets which is probably scarce, verifiable, and without troubles transferable. In this bankruptcy, we are able to discover the numerous factors of accumulating and making an investment in NFT creative endeavors.

One of the essential factor sights for lenders is the exclusivity that includes owning an NFT artwork. Unlike traditional art work office work, in which more than one copies can exist, each NFT artwork is one-of-a-kind. This scarcity gives price to the piece and makes it tremendously distinguished thru lenders.

Investing in NFT works of art additionally can be financially worthwhile. As greater people apprehend the functionality of those virtual property, their marketplace rate has been at the rise. Some early adopters have visible large returns on their investments as name for for fantastic portions will boom over the years.

However, like each investment, there are risks concerned with reference to amassing and investing in NFT works of art. The marketplace may be risky, with charges fluctuating based totally mostly on factors which encompass artist reputation or developments in the crypto community. It's vital for buyers to behavior thorough research earlier than making any purchases.

When thinking about which NFT works of art to put money into, it's far important to evaluate each the inventive first rate and ancient significance of the piece. Just because of the truth some element is uncommon does no longer constantly advocate it'll maintain lengthy-term price if there isn't call for from clients or a robust imaginative popularity within the lower back of it.

Additionally, information an artist's body of exertions can provide insight into their potential destiny success. Artists who have set up themselves internal traditional art work circles or have a robust on line presence can be more likely to create treasured works that stand the take a look at of time.

Chapter 11: Legal Considerations For Nft

In this bankruptcy, we are able to delve into the legal additives surrounding the possession of Non-Fungible Tokens (NFTs) and the ability copyright troubles that rise up in the digital artwork worldwide. As NFTs advantage recognition, it's far crucial to understand the felony framework that governs their possession and protects artists' rights.

One of the primary worries on the equal time as dealing with NFT possession is establishing a smooth chain of call. Unlike physical works of artwork, which regularly encompass provenance records, tracing an paintings's records may be hard within the virtual realm. However, blockchain generation gives a transparent ledger device that may help installation authenticity and tune ownership transfers.

Copyright problems moreover come into play at the equal time as discussing NFTs. Artists should make certain they've got proper authorization or licensing rights for any copyrighted cloth included into their paintings. This consists of using pictures, track, or distinctive progressive content owned thru 1/three parties. Failure to gain permission have to result in criminal disputes and monetary liabilities.

Additionally, artists want to hold in mind whether or no longer they are selling really one in all a kind rights to their artwork or keeping certain usage rights at the identical time as minting an NFT. It is important to clearly define those phrases inside smart contracts related to every token sale to keep away from misunderstandings or destiny conflicts.

Another aspect properly absolutely well worth considering is international copyright prison guidelines considering that digital art work is aware about no barriers at the internet. Artists want to familiarize themselves with copyright regulations in precise jurisdictions in the event that they intend to sell their NFTs globally.

Furthermore, as lenders accumulate NFTs as investments or for private enjoyment, they need to recognize what precisely they're shopping for beyond in reality proudly proudly owning a completely unique token associated with a bit of virtual art. The terms and situations related to every buy ought to define any obstacles on reproduction rights or commercial use.

It's vital for each artists and lenders alike to seek advice from jail experts who concentrate on highbrow property regulation earlier than conducting vast transactions associated with NFTs. These specialists can provide steering on copyright troubles, licensing agreements, and the crook implications of owning and shopping for and promoting virtual assets.

In end, navigating the jail panorama surrounding NFT ownership and copyright problems is critical for each artists and collectors. Establishing a clear chain of call, obtaining right permissions for copyrighted cloth, defining usage rights inside smart contracts, understanding global copyright jail pointers, and attempting to find criminal advice are all crucial steps to ensure a clean and legally compliant experience in the international of NFTs.

Tokenizing Real-World Assets with NFTs

In this monetary damage, we are able to delve into the exciting global of tokenizing real-global property using Non-Fungible Tokens (NFTs). NFTs have revolutionized the way we apprehend and engage with virtual assets, however their functionality extends a protracted manner past the world of art work. With NFT technology, it's far now possible to tokenize physical assets which encompass real property, expensive objects, intellectual belongings rights, and further.

Tokenization refers back to the procedure of changing a tangible or intangible asset proper into a virtual instance on a blockchain. By doing so, the ones property turn out to be divisible and transferable in a stable and obvious way. This opens up new possibilities for possession, investment opportunities, fractional ownership fashions, and liquidity for historically illiquid property.

One instance of tokenizing real-worldwide assets is through fractional ownership of homes. Imagine being able to put money into excessive-price houses while not having to shop for a whole belongings outright. Through NFTs representing fractions of those homes, shoppers can advantage exposure to beneficial real estate markets that had been previously inaccessible.

Another software lies in tokenizing luxurious items along side wonderful art work portions or uncommon collectibles. By growing unique NFTs tied to those items' provenance and authenticity statistics on the blockchain, proprietors can make sure their investments are real while furthermore permitting smooth transferability between clients and dealers worldwide.

Intellectual property rights are a few distinct area in which NFTs could make a large impact.

Artists can tokenize their creations by using manner of minting them as NFTs on numerous structures. This lets in artists to maintain control over their art work at the equal time as though making the most of its price appreciation thru royalties earned from subsequent earnings.

Furthermore, organizations can rent NFT technology to create loyalty applications or reward systems for clients via issuing distinct tokens that deliver get right of access to to big sports or confined edition products/services.

The advantages of tokenizing real-worldwide property with NFTs enlarge past monetary troubles on my own; moreover they provide increased transparency, protection, and overall performance. Blockchain era guarantees that ownership information are immutable and without issues verifiable, reducing the threat of fraud or disputes.

However, it's miles vital to word that tokenizing real-international belongings with NFTs continues to be a specifically new idea and faces annoying situations. Regulatory frameworks want to be developed to deal with jail concerns surrounding the ones digital representations of bodily belongings. Additionally, ensuring tremendous adoption and information amongst capacity consumers can be essential for the success of this rising marketplace.

In quit, tokenizing real-worldwide belongings with NFTs opens up thrilling opportunities for asset ownership, investment possibilities, fractional ownership models, and liquidity in traditionally illiquid markets. From houses to luxurious goods and highbrow belongings rights, NFTs have the capability to revolutionize how we've got interplay with tangible belongings inside the virtual age. However, similarly exploration and improvement are needed to triumph over regulatory hurdles and make sure extraordinary adoption on this evolving landscape.

The Future Potential of Decentralized Finance (DeFi) with NFTs

Decentralized finance, usually known as DeFi, has been making waves in the global of blockchain era. With its promise of democratizing economic systems and getting rid of intermediaries, DeFi has won sizable interest from buyers and enthusiasts alike. But what feature can Non-Fungible Tokens (NFTs) play in the destiny improvement of DeFi?

NFTs have often been related to virtual art work and collectibles. However, their capability extends a protracted manner past those geographical areas. As we delve into the future opportunities of DeFi with NFTs, it turns into obvious that they might revolutionize numerous elements of decentralized finance.

One area wherein NFTs could make a big effect is in lending and borrowing protocols internal DeFi ecosystems. By tokenizing real-global belongings which encompass real property or expensive gadgets through NFTs, individuals can free up liquidity without counting on traditional banking establishments. This opens up new avenues for collateralization and expands get entry to to credit rating for folks who may not meet traditional necessities.

Moreover, NFT-based totally completely absolutely insurance structures must become a sport-changer within the coverage company inside the realm of decentralized finance. By developing particular tokens representing coverage guidelines or coverage plans, humans can switch hazard amongst themselves without related to standard insurers. Smart contracts embedded inner the ones NFTs ensure obvious claim settlements based mostly on predefined situations.

Another exciting prospect lies in the use of NFTs to fractionalize ownership rights over immoderate-price property like artwork or uncommon collectibles. Fractional possession lets in more than one purchasers to very private a part of an asset represented via an NFT token while profiting from functionality appreciation or apartment income generated through that asset.

Furthermore, integrating recognition systems into DeFi protocols through NFT-based totally completely identity verification mechanisms may additionally need to decorate accept as true with amongst members internal decentralized networks. These popularity scores tied to character wallets might probable allow extra correct chance evaluation even as venture peer-to-peer transactions or lending activities.

The capability for NFTs to disrupt the derivatives marketplace inside DeFi need to not be disregarded. By developing NFTs that constitute spinoff contracts, human beings can exchange and speculate on various underlying assets with out relying on centralized exchanges or intermediaries. This opens up a whole new worldwide of possibilities for decentralized derivatives buying and selling.

Additionally, NFT-based prediction markets may want to grow to be effective system for crowd understanding and forecasting future activities. These markets permit people to shop for and sell tokens representing their predictions approximately unique effects, together with election effects or stock expenses. The collective intelligence collected from those markets can offer valuable insights into future trends and possibilities.

As we find out the destiny capability of DeFi with NFTs, it will become clean that their integration has the strength to reshape traditional economic systems essentially. However, demanding situations which incorporates scalability, interoperability between unique blockchain networks, and regulatory frameworks need to be addressed for huge adoption.

In give up, Non-Fungible Tokens have the capability to revolutionize decentralized finance in severa strategies. From unlocking liquidity through asset tokenization to permitting fractional ownership and enhancing accept as true with thru reputation systems - the opportunities are massive. As generation advances and in addition use instances emerge, we're capable of assume NFTs to play an more and more massive characteristic in shaping the destiny panorama of DeFi.

Navigating the Challenges and Risks in the World of NTFS

In the ever-evolving worldwide of Non-Fungible Tokens (NFTs), there are sure to be annoying conditions and risks that each creators and lenders should navigate. As this digital panorama maintains to extend, it's far critical to understand these functionality pitfalls and extend strategies for mitigating them.

One undertaking lies within the verification process of NFT authenticity. With numerous structures emerging, ensuring that an NFT is actual can be a daunting project. The decentralized nature of blockchain technology has added about a sense of believe, however it additionally opens doors for fraudulent sports sports. It is critical for participants in the NFT market to behavior thorough research on systems, artists, and artistic endeavors earlier than making any purchases or investments.

Another chance entails copyright infringement problems within the realm of NFTs. While blockchain offers transparency and immutability, it does not routinely assure right licensing or possession rights. Artists should take precautions via registering their paintings with applicable copyright authorities and surely pointing out their phrases of use while minting an NFT.

Furthermore, rate volatility poses a large task within the international of NTFS. Just like every other asset elegance, NFT values can differ dramatically primarily based mostly on market call for and inclinations. Collectors need to carefully bear in mind their funding alternatives at the same time as being conscious that expenses might also rise or fall .

The environmental impact associated with sure blockchain networks used for developing NTFS is some other problem genuinely definitely worth addressing. Proof-of-Work (PoW) blockchains devour great portions of electricity within the course of mining tactics that might make a contribution to carbon emissions. Exploring opportunity consensus mechanisms along with Proof-of-Stake (PoS) or environmentally notable blockchains may need to help alleviate those troubles.

Chapter 12: The Intersection Between Traditional Art Market

The artwork international has normally been a realm of creativity, expression, and innovation. Traditionally, artists could probably create physical works of artwork using numerous mediums at the side of paint, sculpture, or photographs. These works may additionally then be displayed in galleries and museums for art work lovers to recognize and purchase.

However, with the advent of virtual era, a trendy shape of artistic expression has emerged - digital art. Digital paintings encompass numerous paperwork like laptop-generated pics, virtual reality opinions, and interactive installations This shift towards the digital medium has unfolded interesting opportunities for artists to discover new techniques and achieve wider audiences.

But what takes region whilst the ones two worlds collide? How does conventional art intersect with the hastily growing virtual paintings marketplace?

One considerable intersection point is the idea of ownership. In the conventional art work market, proudly owning an paintings frequently way owning a physical item that can be displayed in a single's home or gallery area. The price of traditional works of art is frequently determined through factors which incorporates rarity, provenance (the information of ownership), and essential acclaim.

In evaluation, virtual works of artwork exist merely inside the digital realm without a tangible shape. They can be resultseasily reproduced and shared in some unspecified time in the future of more than one systems on line. This will increase questions about how ownership is set up in the context of digital art work.

Enter non-fungible tokens (NFTs). NFTs are precise cryptographic tokens that are stored on blockchain networks like Ethereum. They provide evidence of authenticity and possession for virtual assets which encompass artwork.

By tokenizing their creations via NFTs, artists can set up scarcity within the otherwise infinitely reproducible worldwide of digital paintings. Each NFT represents a selected piece or model inner an artist's frame of exertions.

This intersection amongst conventional and virtual markets permits lenders to diversify their portfolios via the use of making an investment in every physical works of art and digitally local quantities represented with the useful resource of NFTs.

Moreover, this convergence additionally offers opportunities for collaboration amongst artists from awesome backgrounds. Traditional artists can discover virtual mediums and check with new techniques, even as virtual artists can comprise factors of conventional artwork into their creations.

For example, a painter might possibly use digital reality technology to create an immersive revel in for web site visitors, blurring the limits among bodily and digital artwork. Similarly, a virtual artist want to collaborate with a sculptor to hold their artwork to life thru three-D printing.

The intersection among conventional and digital paintings markets furthermore challenges the belief of exclusivity. In the past, get entry to to excessive-profile galleries or museums became limited to a pick out few. However, with the upward thrust of on line structures and social media, artists now have the opportunity to showcase their paintings globally without depending mostly on conventional gatekeepers.

This democratization of get proper of access to has brought on multiplied visibility for growing artists who might not have had the identical opportunities inside the conventional paintings international. It allows them to bring together their very very very own organizations and connect immediately with lenders and fans from round the world.

In stop, as era continues to increase, we find out ourselves at an exciting crossroads in which traditional artwork intersects with the rapidly evolving virtual art work market. This convergence brings forth new opportunities for creative expression, ownership models via NFTs, collaboration between distinct mediums, and extra accessibility for each creators and audiences alike.

As we navigate this intersection collectively, it is crucial that we encompass innovation while preserving the center values that make artwork this shape of powerful force in our society - creativity, authenticity, and human connection.

Merging Physical and Digital Worlds through Augmented Reality (AR)

Augmented Reality (AR) has emerged as a powerful device that bridges the distance some of the bodily and digital geographical areas, developing immersive opinions that blend virtual elements with our real-worldwide surroundings. This financial ruin explores how AR is revolutionizing diverse industries and remodeling the manner we interact with paintings, amusement, education, and further.

In contemporary years, AR era has advanced with the resource of leaps and bounds, permitting us to overlay laptop-generated pics onto our view of the physical international. Through the use of smartphones or specialized headsets, users can now enjoy a present day-day layer of truth in which digital items seamlessly coexist with their instantaneous surroundings.

One location in which AR is making large strides is in the realm of artwork. Artists are harnessing this era to create interactive installations that invite website visitors to have interaction with their art work on an entire new stage. Imagine taking walks into an empty gallery region only to appearance colorful artwork come alive earlier than your eyes or sculptures morphing into one-of-a-kind paperwork as you drift spherical them. With AR, artists can move past conventional barriers and loose up limitless opportunities for creativity.

Entertainment industries also are embracing AR as a manner to enhance consumer reports. From cellular gaming applications that superimpose virtual characters onto real-worldwide settings to live performances providing holographic projections interacting with human performers, augmented fact adds a similarly layer of pleasure and immersion.

Education is every different situation making the maximum of merging physical and digital worlds thru AR. Students can find out historic internet internet sites genuinely or dissect complex medical ideas the usage of interactive 3-D models projected onto their textbooks. By bringing summary thoughts into tangible visualizations internal their instantaneous environment, studying becomes more engaging and awesome.

Moreover, groups are leveraging augmented truth for advertising skills. Companies can create unique brand research thru protecting product facts or promotional content fabric at once onto physical packaging or storefronts the use of markers diagnosed via the usage of AR-enabled gadgets. This no longer pleasant captures clients' hobby but moreover offers precious insights into purchaser behavior and options.

While the ability of AR is extensive, there are even though traumatic situations to overcome. Technical boundaries, which include tool compatibility and processing strength, want to be addressed for wonderful adoption. Additionally, privateness issues rise up as AR blurs the line amongst public and private areas.

Nonetheless, the merging of bodily and virtual worlds through augmented fact opens up a realm of opportunities which have been once constrained to our imagination. As era maintains to boom, we're capable of count on even greater seamless integration among the ones nation-states, remodeling how we understand and interact with our environment.

In stop, augmented truth has emerge as a catalyst for merging bodily and digital worlds. It empowers artists to push barriers in their innovative expressions while improving leisure reports for audiences. Education advantages from immersive studying environments created via manner of overlaying virtual content material onto real-global settings. Businesses find out new strategies to interact clients via interactive advertising and advertising campaigns. As we navigate this interesting frontier of era, it is vital to deal with demanding situations on the identical time as embracing the limitless opportunities that AR brings forth in bridging realities like in no way earlier than.

Evolving Trends in Crypto-Art Collections

In the ever-converting panorama of virtual paintings, crypto-paintings collections have emerged as a fascinating and evolving fashion. These collections aren't simplest reshaping the manner we recognize and recognize art work but moreover revolutionizing the idea of ownership and price.

One of the vital aspect inclinations in crypto-paintings collections is the rise of decentralized marketplaces. These structures leverage blockchain era to permit artists to immediately connect with creditors, putting off intermediaries and taking into account introduced transparency. This shift has democratized get proper of get entry to to to paintings, empowering growing artists who may additionally have previously struggled to benefit popularity within conventional paintings circles.

Another extremely good trend is the integration of digital truth (VR) into crypto-artwork evaluations. By immersing visitors in digital environments, VR complements engagement and offers a totally specific angle on artistic endeavors. Collectors can now explore digital galleries from everywhere within the worldwide, growing an immersive experience that transcends physical barriers.

Additionally, collaborations amongst artists and technologists have given shipping to revolutionary styles of interactive crypto-paintings installations. Through augmented fact (AR), the ones installations combination digital elements with real-worldwide environment, blurring the limits between physical area and virtual creations. This fusion creates captivating reminiscences that captivate audiences whilst pushing modern barriers.

Furthermore, fractional ownership has obtained traction inside crypto-paintings collections. With this version, more than one people can collectively very non-public a fragment of an paintings thru tokenization on blockchain networks. Fractional possession permits for broader participation in excessive-price artistic endeavors which have been as fast as one-of-a-kind to wealthy lenders or institutions.

The emergence of non-fungible tokens (NFTs) has also completed a large function in shaping dispositions inside crypto-artwork collections. NFTs provide evidence of authenticity and region of records for everybody artwork or collectible object they represent on blockchain networks like Ethereum. Artists can tokenize their works as NFTs, permitting solid transactions even as retaining provenance digitally.

Social media structures have come to be instrumental in promoting and showcasing crypto-artwork collections. Artists and lenders can leverage those structures to percentage their works, advantage publicity, and hook up with a worldwide goal marketplace. The viral nature of social media has propelled the recognition of crypto-artwork, growing new opportunities for artists to monetize their creations.

Moreover, sustainability has emerged as an critical interest in crypto-artwork collections. As blockchain networks eat big quantities of electricity due to mining strategies, artists and creditors are exploring possibility answers that lower environmental effect. Some obligations embody using evidence-of-stake blockchains or offsetting carbon emissions generated via NFT transactions.

In quit, evolving tendencies in crypto-paintings collections preserve to reshape the artwork global as we apprehend it. Decentralized marketplaces, digital truth reviews, interactive installations, fractional ownership fashions, non-fungible tokens (NFTs), social media advertising, and sustainability concerns are all contributing factors using this modification. As generation advances and modern minds push boundaries in addition, we're capable of anticipate even extra interesting developments inside the realm of crypto-paintings collections.

Chapter 13: Diversifying Revenue Streams

Artists have lengthy relied on the sale in their proper works of art as a primary deliver of profits. However, within the virtual age, in which artwork may be effortlessly reproduced and shared online, artists face new stressful conditions in monetizing their creations. One modern solution that has emerged is the concept of royalties from resales.

Traditionally, while an artist sells an paintings, they gather price great for that initial transaction. If the paintings later appreciates in price and is resold thru a collector or gallery, the artist does now not benefit financially from this secondary market interest. This loss of ongoing reimbursement can be irritating for artists who see their works increase in fee through the years.

Enter royalties from resales — a mechanism that lets in artists to earn a percent of subsequent income of their innovative endeavors. This machine ensures that artists keep to profits even after their initial sale and offers them with a greater sustainable sales movement.

The implementation of resale royalties varies throughout different jurisdictions and systems. Some global locations have added law mandating resale royalty rights for visible artists, ensuring they get maintain of a detail (usually round four%) of any destiny profits concerning their works. These laws aim to defend artists' interests and well known the continued price they carry about to the art market.

In addition to jail frameworks, online platforms committed to promoting NFTs have moreover embraced resale royalties as part of their industrial organization models. These systems robotically implement smart contracts that allocate a percent of every resale again to the original artist or writer. This technique creates transparency and be given as proper with in the market at the same time as incentivizing creditors to assist rising know-how.

Diversifying income streams through royalties from resales gives numerous benefits for artists past sincerely monetary benefit:

1) Recognition: By receiving ongoing reimbursement for resales, artists are said for his or her contribution to shaping cultural dispositions and progressive actions.

2) Sustainability: Royalties offer stability amidst fluctuating artwork markets with the aid of the usage of manner of making a regular earnings glide that can guide artists in some unspecified time inside the future of lean intervals.

3) Long-time period Investment: Artists can view their artworks as lengthy-time period investments, know-how that they may keep to benefit from any destiny appreciation in charge.

four) Support for Emerging Artists: Resale royalties encourage creditors to spend money on emerging artists, information that their useful resource will immediately contribute to the artist's success.

However, it's miles crucial to be conscious that enforcing resale royalties also will growth a few stressful conditions. Determining the right percent of royalties and ensuring effective enforcement mechanisms require cautious attention. Additionally, there may be resistance from excessive exceptional segments of the art work market who argue toward potential boundaries on loose exchange.

Nonetheless, with the upward push of NFTs and blockchain generation permitting apparent transactions and clever contracts, the implementation of resale royalties has end up more feasible than ever in advance than. This revolutionary approach no longer nice benefits man or woman artists but additionally contributes to a extra equitable and sustainable art environment.

In cease, diversifying sales streams for artists via royalties from resales represents an exciting opportunity inside the digital age. By embracing this model, artists can steady ongoing financial reimbursement on the identical time as gaining reputation for his or her contributions to the art work worldwide. As we navigate this new era of virtual artwork and assets ownership, it's miles vital to discover revolutionary strategies to beneficial resource creators and make certain their endured success.

Celebrity Endorsements & Collaborations in the World Of NTFS

In the ever-evolving global of Non-Fungible Tokens (NFTs), one style that has received first rate traction is movie megastar endorsements and collaborations. Celebrities from diverse fields, which include song, film, sports activities sports activities, and fashion, have embraced NFTs as a technique to have interaction with their enthusiasts in new and interesting processes.

The involvement of celebrities within the NFT place brings attention and credibility to this rising technology. By associating themselves with NFT responsibilities or growing their private particular tokens, celebrities can tap into their huge fan bases and create a proper away connection among themselves and their supporters.

One manner celebrities are leveraging NFTs is through presenting specific virtual content cloth fabric or reports. For example, a musician can also launch limited edition songs or albums as NFTs, permitting fanatics to private a piece of music information. Similarly, an actor might also want to auction off within the decrease returned of-the-scenes photographs or memorabilia from a loved movie franchise.

These film big name-endorsed NFTs not exceptional offer lovers with particular collectibles but also serve as a shape of authentication. Owning an NFT associated with a specific film celebrity offers rate and standing to the token itself. It will become greater than best a digital asset; it becomes a image of fandom and manual for that specific artist or athlete.

Collaborations among celebrities and artists in the global of NTFS have moreover become increasingly more commonplace. Artists who focus on growing digital art often crew up with well-known personalities to deliver exquisite quantities that integrate each innovative imaginative and prescient and big call electricity. These collaborations bring about extensively sought-after works of art that appeal to creditors from round the sector.

Moreover, the ones partnerships amplify past visible paintings into exceptional innovative realms which embody style layout or virtual truth research. Celebrities convey their particular fashion and impact to those collaborations at the same time as artists make a contribution their technical know-how in crafting immersive digital environments.

The impact of celebrity involvement is going beyond just financial profits for both activities. It allows to bridge the space among traditional amusement industries and the digital art international, fostering innovation and pushing boundaries. By embracing NFTs, celebrities are not most effective growing their personal brand however additionally contributing to the increase and recognition of this new shape of creative expression.

However, it is important to phrase that celebrity endorsements and collaborations inside the world of NTFS include their straightforward proportion of demanding situations. As with any growing generation, there are risks involved, which include capacity scams or fraudulent sports sports. It is vital for every celebrities and lovers to exercising caution while challenge NFT transactions.

In conclusion, celeb endorsements and collaborations have come to be an essential part of the NFT landscape. They supply interest, credibility, and particular opportunities for fans to connect to their preferred stars on a deeper diploma. Through unique content cloth cloth offerings and revolutionary partnerships, celebrities contribute to the increase and evolution of NFTs at the same time as simultaneously developing their non-public acquire inside the digital realm.

Nurturing Creativity through Community Engagement Platforms

In this bankruptcy, we are able to discover the energy of community engagement structures in fostering and nurturing creativity in the realm of non-fungible tokens (NFTs). These structures function digital areas in which artists, lenders, and lovers come together to proportion ideas, collaborate on duties, and assist every different's creative endeavors.

Community engagement structures play a vital position in developing an surroundings that encourages innovative expression. They offer a area for artists to expose off their paintings and get keep of remarks from a supportive community. By connecting with like-minded individuals who recognize their artistry, creators benefit notion and motivation to push their barriers similarly.

One such platform is ArtConnect—a thriving on-line network in which artists can hook up with friends, curators, and creditors. Artists can create profiles showcasing their portfolios while mission discussions about various factors of paintings introduction. This platform fosters collaboration by way of way of allowing artists to locate capacity collaborators for joint initiatives or exhibitions.

Another top notch instance is SuperRare—an one-of-a-kind digital art work market that operates on blockchain generation. It permits artists to mint restricted-version NFTs in their art work to be had on the market at the same time as imparting creditors with get proper of entry to to unique quantities they may private digitally. The platform furthermore permits direct conversation among creators and customers via feedback sections or private messages.

These network engagement structures now not handiest facilitate connections however additionally provide academic property for aspiring artists. Many host webinars, workshops, or tutorials performed through the usage of established experts inside the difficulty. This permits growing abilties to investigate new strategies or advantage insights into the industry from professional practitioners.

Moreover, those systems often arrange competitions or demanding conditions that encourage members to push their creative limitations similarly. Such sports foster wholesome opposition among artists at the same time as supplying possibilities for recognition and exposure in the network.

The impact of these systems extends beyond person artist boom; they contribute appreciably to the general improvement of virtual art work as a whole. By bringing collectively severa perspectives and patterns from spherical the area onto one accessible platform, those agencies foster a rich and colorful innovative atmosphere.

Through community engagement structures, artists can collect valuable remarks from their friends, advantage exposure to new thoughts and strategies, and find out help of their innovative journey. These structures feature catalysts for innovation with the aid of nurturing an environment that encourages experimentation and collaboration.

In surrender, community engagement structures play a critical characteristic in nurturing creativity inside the global of non-fungible tokens. They provide areas wherein artists can connect to like-minded people, display off their paintings, collaborate on tasks, and study from each super. By fostering an inclusive and supportive surroundings, those systems make a contribution to the increase of character artists at the same time as enriching the digital paintings landscape as a whole.

The Environmental Impact of Proof-of-Work Blockchains

In current years, there was developing state of affairs about the environmental impact of evidence-of-artwork blockchains. These blockchain networks, including Bitcoin and Ethereum, rely on a consensus mechanism that calls for miners to resolve complicated mathematical puzzles if you want to validate transactions and upload them to the blockchain.

The method of fixing those puzzles requires large computational strength and strength intake. As a give up end result, the carbon footprint associated with mining cryptocurrencies has turn out to be a subject of dialogue and scrutiny.

One important environmental assignment surrounding proof-of-paintings blockchains is their excessive electricity consumption. The computational strength required for mining operations consequences in an huge name for for energy. This name for regularly results in elevated reliance on fossil fuels, contributing to greenhouse fuel emissions and exacerbating weather change.

Furthermore, the growing recognition of cryptocurrencies has introduced about a surge in mining sports activities spherical the sector. Mining farms prepared with powerful hardware devour huge quantities of strength on a each day basis. In some times, these farms are placed in areas in which coal or different non-renewable electricity assets are frequent, similarly intensifying their environmental impact.

To located matters into attitude, it's miles predicted that Bitcoin on my own consumes greater power than whole global places like Argentina or Switzerland. This spectacular statistic highlights the pressing need for sustainable alternatives inside the blockchain agency.

Efforts are being made by using the usage of researchers and developers to deal with the ones issues through numerous manner. One capability solution is transitioning from proof-of-paintings (PoW) consensus mechanisms to alternative models like proof-of-stake (PoS). Unlike PoW systems that require miners to compete in the direction of every amazing the use of computational power, PoS relies on validators who hold gift coins within the community.

By disposing of beneficial useful resource-in depth mining operations from the equation, PoS blockchains considerably reduce strength consumption and carbon emissions associated with transaction validation techniques.

Another approach includes exploring renewable electricity belongings for powering mining operations. Some in advance-questioning groups have already started out putting in sun-powered or hydroelectric-powered mining farms, aiming to lessen their carbon footprint.

Additionally, technological upgrades in hardware usual performance and optimization can make a contribution to reducing the power necessities of blockchain networks. As era evolves, extra strength-inexperienced mining tool is being advanced, that can probably alleviate a number of the environmental problems associated with proof-of-paintings blockchains.

It's vital for the blockchain community as a whole to apprehend and address these environmental demanding conditions. By embracing sustainable practices and exploring opportunity consensus mechanisms, we're capable of mitigate the poor effect on our planet at the identical time as however taking part inside the blessings that blockchain generation gives.

In end, the environmental problems surrounding proof-of-paintings blockchains are large. The excessive strength consumption and reliance on non-renewable resources enhance valid questions about sustainability. However, through innovation and collective efforts inside the company, there's desire for locating answers that balance each technological improvement and ecological obligation. It's crucial for stakeholders to collaborate towards developing a greener destiny for blockchain technology.

Chapter 14: The Impact Of Social Media

In contemporary digital age, social media systems have come to be an essential a part of our lives. They be a part of us with friends, family, or perhaps strangers from round the arena. But beyond personal connections, social media has moreover performed a huge characteristic in shaping tendencies and influencing various industries. One such enterprise that has skilled the profound effect of social media is the area of Non-Fungible Tokens (NFTs).

Social media systems provide artists and creators with a effective device to expose off their artwork to a global target market. With only a few clicks, artists can proportion their NFT creations across multiple structures like Instagram, Twitter, TikTok, and extra. This at once accessibility permits for remarkable publicity and visibility.

The viral nature of social media amplifies the obtain capability for NFTs exponentially. When an artist's art work is going viral on those structures due to its location of expertise or cultural relevance, it creates a ripple effect that spreads in some unspecified time inside the destiny of the net community. People begin sharing and discussing these creative endeavors inner their networks, generating buzz and interest.

Moreover, influencers play a essential characteristic in riding interest in NFTs thru their large followings on social media structures. Influencers are human beings who have mounted credibility inside precise niches or groups on line. By endorsing or promoting high-quality NFT obligations or collections to their followership base, they are able to significantly have an impact on market developments.

Another manner social media affects the popularity of NFTs is thru fostering businesses centered around this growing technology. Online businesses committed to discussing all subjects related to NFTs have sprung up during diverse structures like Reddit or

Discord channels in which fans accumulate to percentage insights about new releases or communicate funding strategies.

Furthermore, many artists leverage social media as a way for engaging immediately with their enthusiasts and lenders thru live streams or Q&A education. This degree of interaction fosters deeper connections among creators and customers on the equal time as moreover supplying valuable feedback for artists to refine their craft.

However, it is crucial to study that social media's influence on NFTs isn't with out its annoying conditions. The speedy-paced nature of those structures can once in a while result in a saturation of content material fabric, making it greater tough for man or woman artists to stand out amidst the noise. Additionally, the hype-driven nature of social media trends may additionally additionally create quick-lived spikes in interest that aren't sustainable in the end.

In give up, social media has undeniably performed a large feature in the usage of the popularity and adoption of NFTs. Its functionality to attach artists with worldwide audiences, facilitate viral sharing, and empower influencers has propelled this rising era into mainstream focus. However, as with each style inspired through social media, it's far critical for creators and creditors alike to navigate through the noise and focus on building significant connections interior this ever-evolving panorama.

Chapter 15: Integrating Smart Contracts

Smart contracts, powered via blockchain technology, have the capability to revolutionize severa factors of our each day lives. These self-executing contracts are designed to robotically put into effect the terms and situations agreed upon through the use of all sports worried. By getting rid of intermediaries and counting on decentralized networks, clever contracts provide transparency, safety, and usual overall performance in a sizable form of packages.

One region wherein smart contracts may want to make a exquisite impact is in the realm of real assets transactions. Traditionally, looking for or promoting belongings consists of severa intermediaries collectively with criminal experts, marketers, and banks. This approach may be time-eating and pricey. However, with smart contracts, those intermediaries can be modified with the resource of manner of code that guarantees seamless execution of agreements among purchasers and dealers.

Imagine buying a house without having to rely upon more than one parties for verification and transfer of possession. With smart contracts included into actual property transactions, the device will become streamlined. The settlement may automatically verify the customer's price range thru virtual overseas money payments whilst simultaneously shifting possession rights as soon as all situations are met.

But it does not save you there - clever contracts have the ability to transform unique areas too! Take deliver chain manipulate for instance. Tracking goods from their basis to excursion spot often consists of complex place of business paintings and guide strategies susceptible to errors or frauds. By integrating smart contracts into deliver chains the usage of era like Internet-of-Things (IoT) gadgets or RFID tags, we're capable of create an immutable record of every step along the way.

These tamper-proof records make sure transparency at each diploma - from production to distribution - lowering inefficiencies and growing take delivery of as true with among stakeholders worried in worldwide change networks. Additionally, computerized rate systems inside the ones smart settlement-enabled supply chains dispose of delays attributable to traditional banking strategies.

Another thrilling software lies in healthcare offerings wherein affected man or woman information privacy is vital however hard because of centralized garage structures prone to breaches. By leveraging blockchain-powered smart contracts for medical facts manipulate, sufferers advantage control over their non-public facts. They can provide get right of get entry to to to healthcare agencies on the equal time as retaining ownership and privacy rights.

Moreover, clever contracts can automate coverage claims processing, reducing the time and effort required for verification. Claims is probably routinely evaluated primarily based on predefined standards, making sure faster payouts to policyholders in times of want.

The integration of clever contracts into normal existence moreover extends to areas along with vote casting systems, energy grids, highbrow property management, or even non-public finance. The possibilities are splendid!

However, it's essential to widely known that integrating smart contracts into everyday life comes with its very own set of stressful conditions. Regulatory frameworks want to conform to address this rising generation at the identical time as addressing problems associated with safety, privateness, and criminal enforceability.

In quit, the integration of smart contracts into our every day lives has the capability to revolutionize severa industries by streamlining strategies and growing transparency. From real assets transactions to supply chain manage and healthcare offerings - the benefits are large. As we navigate this new technology of decentralized technology, embracing clever contracts opens up a global of opportunities for human beings and businesses alike.

Navigating Intellectual Property Rights in a Digital Era

In this chapter, we delve into the complicated realm of highbrow assets rights (IPR) and the manner they'll be impacted through using the arrival of the digital era. As generation continues to boom at an remarkable pace, it has grow to be increasingly more tough to guard and implement IPR in a global in which statistics can be without troubles shared and reproduced.

The digital age has delivered approximately new stressful conditions for creators, artists, and innovators who depend on their highbrow creations for recognition and financial gain. With the rise of non-fungible tokens (NFTs), which permit for unique possession of virtual assets, questions surrounding copyright infringement, sincere use, and licensing have grow to be greater ordinary than ever earlier than.

One of the important thing troubles confronted in navigating IPR in a digital technology is figuring out what constitutes originality. In conventional forms of paintings or innovation, it have end up mainly sincere to set up authorship or possession. However, with the convenience of copying and dispensing virtual content material on-line, distinguishing among real creations and replicas has grow to be more and more tough.

Furthermore, as NFTs advantage recognition as a way to shop for and promote virtual ingenious endeavors or collectibles securely the usage of blockchain era, troubles get up concerning unauthorized reproductions or counterfeit items being presented beneath fake pretenses. The task lies no longer great in figuring out those infringements however moreover in enforcing jail motion in opposition to the ones accountable.

To address those stressful conditions correctly requires collaboration amongst creators themselves alongside aspect criminal specialists focusing on intellectual property law. It is essential for artists to recognize their rights whilst growing works that can be at risk of replication or misuse in the massive expanse of cyberspace.

Education plays a crucial position as well; each creators and customers want to be aware about copyright jail suggestions governing severa jurisdictions globally. Additionally, structures internet internet web hosting NFT marketplaces ought to placed into effect robust mechanisms that affirm authenticity even as respecting privateness rights.

As we navigate thru this evolving landscape collectively—in which creativity intersects with generation—it will become imperative to strike a balance amongst protecting intellectual belongings rights and fostering innovation. The virtual era presents each possibilities and demanding situations, and it's far our collective duty to ensure that creators are duly identified for their contributions even as selling an surroundings conducive to inventive expression.

In quit, the virtual technology has introduced approximately huge modifications in how we understand and defend highbrow assets rights. With the upward thrust of NFTs and the benefit of sharing virtual content material cloth material, it's miles critical for creators, clients, and criminal experts alike to conform to this new panorama. By records copyright prison suggestions, enforcing sturdy verification mechanisms, and fostering collaboration inside the present day community, we're able to navigate these demanding situations efficaciously at the identical time as retaining the integrity of intellectual creations in a digital international.

Chapter 16: Fashion Industry Embracing Nfts

The style commercial enterprise business enterprise, recognized for its ordinary pursuit of innovation and trendsetting, has now set its sights on embracing the arena of Non-Fungible Tokens (NFTs). This virtual revolution is reworking the manner we perceive and have interaction with style, providing new possibilities for designers, manufacturers, and clients alike.

In this chapter, we are capable of discover how the fashion organisation is leveraging NFT generation to create specific digital property that redefine possession and authenticity. From virtual fashion shows to constrained version digital apparel collections, let's delve into the thrilling methods wherein NFTs are reshaping the destiny of fashion.

One of the important issue benefits that NFTs convey to the fashion agency is their functionality to set up verifiable shortage. By minting a restricted amount of digital garments or accessories as NFTs on blockchain structures, designers can create exquisite quantities that creditors can truly personal. These virtual gadgets may be bought, offered, or maybe traded similar to physical luxury gadgets.

Moreover, NFTs permit for exceptional creativity in terms of format possibilities. Fashion designers aren't restrained via bodily materials or production limitations. They can test with avant-garde concepts and push limitations without demanding about practicality or manufacturing constraints. The most effective restriction is their creativeness.

Virtual fashion suggests have additionally received traction inside the enterprise way to NFT era. Designers can display off their cutting-edge day creations via immersive digital reviews in which attendees can view and interact with digitally rendered fashions carrying those unique designs. This now not fine reduces expenses related to traditional runway suggests however furthermore opens up new avenues for worldwide accessibility and inclusivity.

Brands are recognizing the ability marketing charge that comes from taking element with influential artists in creating super NFT collections. By partnering with renowned creators who've a robust following inner each artwork and fashion corporations, producers advantage exposure to new audiences while including an element of reputation to their offerings.

For clients, proudly owning an unique virtual fashion object has turn out to be a way to specific their individuality and participate inside the evolving style landscape. NFTs permit them to curate their virtual wardrobes, mixture and in shape virtual garments, and exhibit their precise fashion on social media structures.

However, as with every emerging era, challenges exist within the intersection of NFTs and style. Questions regarding sustainability upward thrust up due to the strength intake related to blockchain networks. Additionally, issues surrounding copyright safety and intellectual assets rights want to be addressed to make certain sincere reimbursement for designers and artists.

Despite the ones challenges, it's far smooth that NFTs have unfolded a modern day realm of possibilities for the style industry. The fusion of artwork, generation, and fashion has created an thrilling vicinity wherein creativity is aware of no bounds. As we go along with the float beforehand into this digital technology of favor, one factor is superb: Non-Fungible Tokens are right right here to stay.

In quit, the adoption of NFTs through the style business enterprise represents a paradigm shift in how we apprehend possession and fee within the international of apparel and accessories. From restrained model virtual collections to immersive digital opinions, NFTs offer endless opportunities for innovation inner this ever-evolving agency. As designers maintain to push boundaries and clients embody this new shape of self-expression via digital fashion devices, we are capable of expect even extra integration among NFT technology and the sector of excessive-prevent couture.

Leveraging Virtual Reality for Enhanced User Experiences

Virtual reality (VR) has emerged as a groundbreaking generation that has the potential to revolutionize numerous industries, which incorporates art work, enjoyment, gaming, or maybe schooling. By immersing clients in a simulated surroundings, VR gives an extraordinary degree of engagement and interactivity.

One place in which VR without a doubt shines is in improving consumer testimonies. Whether it's far exploring digital paintings galleries or embarking on interesting adventures in immersive games, VR takes us beyond the restrictions of the bodily world and transports us into new geographical regions of possibility.

In the region of virtual artwork, VR lets in artists to create three-dimensional masterpieces that may be professional from each perspective. Users can step interior these virtual worlds and engage with inventive endeavors like in no manner in advance than. Imagine strolling via a surreal landscape created through way of an artist's imagination or getting up near have a test complicated statistics of a sculpture – all inside the consolation of your own home.

But it'd no longer prevent at visual arts. Virtual reality moreover holds big capacity for reinforcing storytelling memories. With VR headsets, customers can become active members in narratives in preference to passive observers. They can find out fantastical geographical areas along characters or witness historic activities unfold proper in advance than their eyes.

Gaming is any other place where digital truth has made giant strides in the direction of delivering unforgettable reviews. Instead of truely controlling characters on a display, game enthusiasts are absolutely immersed in recreation worlds wherein they might bodily circulate round and engage with gadgets the usage of movement controllers or haptic feedback devices. This degree of immersion brings video video games to existence like in no way before – making you enjoy like you are sincerely indoors the sport itself.

Education is but some different situation that stands to advantage substantially from leveraging virtual reality era. Students can embark on virtual difficulty trips to ancient landmarks or faraway planets with out leaving their school rooms. They may have interaction with interactive simulations that permit them to exercising actual-international skills in consistent environments on the identical time as receiving instant remarks.

The possibilities are limitless almost approximately leveraging virtual fact for extra acceptable client tales. From education simulations for experts to healing applications in healthcare, VR has the capability to transform how we have a observe, create, and have interaction with virtual content material.

However, it's miles essential to phrase that digital truth stays a unexpectedly evolving generation. As it maintains to boost, we want to address traumatic situations which consist of motion contamination and the need for greater a great deal less pricey and available hardware. Additionally, ethical issues surrounding information privacy and dependancy need to be cautiously examined as VR will become extra blanketed into our daily lives.

In give up, digital reality offers an exciting frontier for boosting man or woman reviews in some unspecified time in the future of severa industries. Whether it is through immersive paintings exhibitions or interactive gaming adventures, VR has the energy to transport us past the confines of our physical worldwide and into geographical regions confined simplest thru creativeness. As technology maintains to improvement, we are able to anticipate even more modern programs of virtual truth as a manner to redefine how we've interaction with digital content within the destiny.

Chapter 17: Educational Applications

Education has usually been a critical pillar of society, shaping the minds and abilities of people. With the advent of non-fungible tokens (NFTs), new possibilities have emerged to revolutionize the academic panorama. NFTs can be executed in severa procedures to enhance analyzing research, sell engagement, and offer particular educational assets.

One progressive software of NFTs in training is the advent of digital certificates or diplomas. Traditionally, those credentials are issued on paper and can be without trouble out of place or forged. By tokenizing them as NFTs on a blockchain, they become tamper-proof and effortlessly verifiable via employers or institutions searching out to validate an character's qualifications.

Furthermore, NFTs may be used to praise university students for their achievements and improvement. Instead of traditional grades or factors systems, educators can assign unique tokens that constitute particular accomplishments or milestones. These tokens may additionally need to then be accrued with the aid of manner of students and exchanged for tangible rewards which consist of books, get proper of entry to to essential sports, or perhaps scholarships.

Another thrilling issue is the capability to create interactive mastering reviews via augmented fact (AR) the use of NFTs. Imagine university college students being capable of check an NFT with their smartphones or pills and immediately having access to more information about a historic artifact in a museum display off or exploring virtual simulations associated with scientific standards noted in magnificence.

Additionally, teachers can leverage NFT era to create customized getting to know pathways for each scholar primarily based on their individual strengths and pastimes. By assigning one-of-a-type styles of tokens representing diverse topics or talents, educators can tailor instructional content material material especially for every learner's dreams.

Collaboration among college college students is also advanced through the usage of NFTs. Group responsibilities may additionally moreover need to involve growing collaborative works of artwork wherein each participant contributes a totally specific element represented through manner of an character token in the very last piece. This now not satisfactory fosters teamwork but additionally permits students to take pleasure of their contributions even as appreciating others' creativity.

Moreover, NFTs may be used to keep and proportion cultural historical past. Historical artifacts or imaginative endeavors which might be hard to physically get admission to or transport may be tokenized as NFTs, allowing people from around the sector to find out and observe them definitely. This opens up new avenues for bypass-cultural statistics and appreciation.

While the educational packages of NFTs keep top notch promise, it's miles critical to cope with potential demanding situations. One scenario is ensuring accessibility for all college college students, irrespective of their socioeconomic backgrounds. Efforts need to be made to bridge the virtual divide and provide same possibilities for reading via NFT technology.

In stop, non-fungible tokens have the functionality to revolutionize schooling by manner of supplying consistent credentials, worthwhile achievements, growing interactive studying reports, personalizing schooling pathways, fostering collaboration among university college students, maintaining cultural history digitally accessible worldwide. As educators maintain exploring those opportunities in a considerate way on the equal time as addressing stressful conditions along the manner we will free up a present day technology of immersive and inclusive education powered thru the usage of NFTs.